Creation Care

D1500658

CHRISTIANITYTODAY

INTERNATIONAL

THOMAS NELSON
Since 1798

NASHVILLE   DALLAS   MEXICO CITY   RIO DE JANEIRO   BEIJING

OTHER BOOKS IN THIS SERIES

Current Issues Bible Study Series: Creation Care
Copyright © 2008 *Christianity Today* International

Editor: Kelli B. Trujillo
Development Editors: Kelli B. Trujillo and Roxanne Wieman
Associate Editor: JoHannah Reardon
Review Editor: David Neff
Page Designer: Robin Crosslin

ISBN 13: 978-1-4185-3413-4

Printed in the United States of America
09 10 11 12 RRD 5 4 3 2 1

CONTENTS

CONTRIBUTING WRITERS

Sheryl Henderson Blunt is a senior news writer for *Christianity Today*.

Wayne Brouwer is senior pastor at Harderwyk Ministries in Holland, Michigan, and the author of *Being a Believer in an Unbelieving World*.

Cindy Crosby is the author of three books, including *By Willoway Brook: Exploring the Landscape of Prayer* (Paraclete), and is editor/compiler of the *Ancient Christian Devotional: A Year of Weekly Readings* (InterVarsity Press).

Andy Crouch is editor of the Christian Vision Project (www.christianvision project.com).

Calvin B. DeWitt is an environmental scientist with the Institute for Environmental Studies at the University of Wisconsin-Madison and director of the Au Sable Institute of Environmental Studies, a Christian center for the integration of biblical teaching and environmental science for college students, professors, and churches. He is the author of *Earth-Wise* (Faith Alive Christian Resources) and the general editor of *The Environment and the Christian* (Baker).

Hunter Farrell lived in Peru as a missionary with his wife and three children for nine years and worked with the Joining Hands Network of Peru. He is now director of Presbyterian World Mission.

Jerone Frame is a contributing author to the website ChristianBibleStudies.com, a service of Christianity Today International.

Helen Turnbull Goody is the communications manager for John Stott Ministries and has written for a variety of publications including *Creation Care* magazine, *Church Web Advisor*, and *Rev.* magazine.

Debbie Gowensmith is the Hawaii Program Director at the Community Conservation Network. She assists communities in identifying and pursuing their goals for environmental restoration.

Joy-Elizabeth Lawrence is a freelance writer. She is also an avid cook, a member of a local CSA farm (Community Supported Agriculture), a shareholder of a dairy herd, and a recent contributor to *Eat Well: A Food Road Map* (published by *culture is not optional).

David N. Livingstone is a professor in the School of GeoSciences at the Queen's University of Belfast. He is the author of *Darwin's Forgotten Defenders* (Eerdmans) and *The Geographical Tradition* (Blackwell).

John E. Silvius is professor of biology at Cedarville (Ohio) University and author of *Biology: Principles and Perspectives*.

Tim Stafford is a senior writer for *Christianity Today* and the author of many books, including *Personal God: Can You Really Know the One Who Made the Universe?* (Zondervan).

Alison Tarka is a stay-at-home mom, blogger, violinist, vegetarian, and freelance writer for small groups; she strives to reduce, reuse, and recycle as much as possible.

Jason Tarka is a pastor in Portland, Oregon where he leads worship, teaches theology, and writes for small groups. He is a bike commuter and a vegetarian.

Kelli B. Trujillo is an editor, author, gardener, recycler, and member of a local organic Community-Supported Agriculture farm near her home in Indianapolis.

Loren Wilkinson is the coauthor, with his wife, Mary Ruth Wilkinson, of *Caring for Creation in Your Own Backyard* (Servant). He teaches at Regent College in Vancouver, British Columbia.

J. Isamu Yamamoto is an author of several books and an editor for Publications International Ltd.

Philip Yancey is editor at large of *Christianity Today* and co-chair of the editorial board for *Books and Culture*. Yancey's most recent book is *Prayer*. His other books include *Rumors of Another World, Reaching for the Invisible God, What's So Amazing About Grace?, Where Is God When It Hurts?*, and many others.

INTRODUCTION

Environmentalism. For some, this is a dirty word. It smacks of political maneuvering and brings to mind New Age tree-huggers or doomsday documentaries. But the divide between the church and environmentalists is narrowing as more and more evangelicals are getting involved in environmental issues as a direct result of their Christian faith. In fact, some top leaders of prominent conservation organizations are committed followers of Jesus Christ. Instead of the term "environmentalism" which is rife with stereotypes and other baggage, these Christians use the term "creation care" to affirm their belief in our Creator and their desire to be good caretakers of the world God has entrusted to us. As the headlines cry out about global warming, diminishing oil reserves, pollution, rainforest destruction, species extinction, and other environmental issues, Christians are engaging these matters through direct action, in their daily choices, and by speaking out.

What about you? How will you care for God's creation? This *Current Issues Bible Study* is designed to facilitate lively and engaging discussion on various facets of this topic and how it connects to our lives as Jesus's followers. As you explore the topic of creation care together, we hope this *Current Issues Bible Study* will help you grow closer as a group and challenge you in ways you may not expect.

For Small Groups

These studies are designed to be used in small groups—communities of people with a commitment to and connection with each other. Whether you're an existing small group or you're just planning to meet for the next eight weeks, this resource will help you deepen your personal faith and grow closer with each other.

On SmallGroups.com, you'll find everything you need to successfully run a small-groups ministry. The insightful, free articles and theme-specific downloads provide expert training. The reproducible curriculum courses bring thought leaders from across the world into your group's discussion at a fraction of the price. And the revolutionary SmallGroupsConnect social network will help keep your group organized and connected 24/7.

Christianity Today Articles

Each study session begins with one or two thought-provoking articles from *Christianity Today* or one of its sister publications. These articles are meant to help you dive deeply into the topic and engage with a variety of thoughts and opinions. Be sure to read the articles before you arrive to your small group meeting; the time you invest on the front-end will greatly enrich your group's discussion. As you read, you may find the articles persuasive and agree heartily with their conclusions; other times you may disagree with the claims of an article, but that's great too. We want these articles to serve as a springboard for lively discussion, so differences in opinion are welcome. For more insightful articles from *Christianity Today* magazine, visit www.ctilibrary.com and subscribe now.

Timing

These studies are designed to be flexible, with plenty of discussion, activities, and prayer time to fill a full small group meeting. If you'd like, you can zero in on a few questions or teaching points and discuss them in greater depth, or you can aim to spend a few minutes on each question of a given session. Be sure to manage your time so that you're able to spend time on the "Going Forward" questions and prayer time at the end of each study.

Ground Rules

True spiritual growth happens in the context of a vibrant Christian community. To establish that type of community in your small group, we recommend a few *ground rules.*

- *Guarantee confidentiality.* Promise together that whatever is said in the context of your small group meeting is *kept* there. This sense of trust and safety will enable you to more honestly share your spiritual struggles.

- *Participate—with balance.* We all have different personalities. Some of us like to talk . . . a lot. Others of us prefer to be quiet. But for this study to truly benefit your group, everyone needs to participate. Make it a personal goal to answer (aloud) at least half of the discussion questions in a given session. This will allow space for others to talk (lest you dominate discussion too much) but will also guarantee your own contribution is made to the discussion (from which other group members will benefit).

- *Be an attentive listener—to each other and to God.* As you read Scripture and discuss these important cultural issues, focus with care and love on the other members of your group. These questions are designed to be open-ended and to allow for a diversity of opinion. Be gracious toward others who express views that are different than your own. And even more important, prayerfully remain attentive to the presence of God speaking to and guiding your group through the Holy Spirit.

It is our prayer that this *Current Issues Bible Study* will change the lives of your group members as you seek to integrate your faith into the environmental issues we face everyday. May the Holy Spirit work in and through your group as you challenge and encourage each other in spiritual growth.

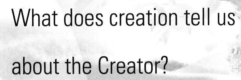

What does creation tell us about the Creator?

SCRIPTURE FOCUS	
	Job 38:4–41:34
	Psalm 19:1–4
	John 1:1–4
	Romans 1:20

RESPECT
FOR THE MAKER

■

Looking up at a dazzling nightscape filled with
stars, you pause and consider how vast and amazing
God is. Examining the intricate pattern of veins on
a leaf, you're reminded of God's artistry and design.
Standing on a summit after a hike, you survey the
land before you and are struck with wonder—you feel
you can sense God's presence. In "The God Who Can't
Be Tamed," Philip Yancey challenges us to live as if
we believe that God uses his creation to point us to
himself. He suggests that if we continue to destroy the
world around us, we will take away opportunities for
people to see evidence of who God is.

■ Before You Meet

Read "The God Who Can't Be Tamed" by Philip Yancey from *Christianity Today*.

THE GOD WHO CAN'T BE TAMED

Could we be losing more than the land when we destroy it?

by Philip Yancey

In what she later called "the most transporting pleasure of my life on the farm," Isak Dinesen went flying across the unspoiled plains of Africa with her friend Denys Finch Hatton. In the film version of *Out of Africa,* Denys first invited her by saying, "I want to show you the world as God sees it." Indeed, the next few minutes of cinematography come close to presenting exactly that. As the frail Moth airplane soars beyond the escarpment that marks the beginning of the Rift Valley in Kenya, the ground falls abruptly away and the zoom lens captures a glimpse of Eden in the grasslands just below.

Great herds of zebras scatter at the sound of the motor, each group wheeling in unison, as if a single mind controlled the bits of modern art dashing across the plain. Huge giraffes—they seemed so gangly and awkward when standing still—gallop away with exquisite gracefulness. Bounding gazelles, outrunning the larger animals, fill in the edge of the scene.

The world as God sees it—does that phrase merely express some foamy romantic notion, or does it contain truth? The Bible gives intriguing hints. Proverbs tells of the act of Creation, when Wisdom "was the craftsman at his [God's] side . . . filled with delight day after day, rejoicing always in his presence, rejoicing in his whole world" (NIV). The seraphs in Isaiah's vision who declared "the whole earth is full of his glory" could hardly have been referring to human beings—not if the rest of the Book of Isaiah is to be believed. At least God had the glory of Nature then, during that very dark time when Israel faced extinction and Judah slid toward idolatry.

God makes plain how he feels about the animal kingdom in his longest single speech, a magnificent address found at the end of Job. Look closely and you will notice a common thread in the specimens he holds up for Job's edification:

- A lioness hunting her prey
- A mountain goat giving birth in the wilds
- A rogue donkey roaming the salt flats
- An ostrich flapping her useless wings with joy
- A stallion leaping high to paw the air
- A hawk, an eagle, and a raven building their nests on the rocky crags

That's a mere warm up—Zoology 101 in Job's education. From there God advances to the behemoth, a hippo-like creature no one can tame, and the mighty, dragonish leviathan. "Can you make a pet of him like a bird or put him on a leash for your girls?" God asks with a touch of scorn. "The mere sight of him is overpowering. No one is fierce enough to rouse him. Who then is able to stand against me?" (NIV, paraphrase).

Wildness is God's underlying message to Job, the one trait his menagerie all hold in common. God is celebrating those members of his created world that will never be domesticated by human beings. Wild animals bring us down a notch, reminding us of something we'd prefer to forget: our creatureliness. And they also announce to our senses the splendor of an invisible, untamable God.

Several times a week, I run among such wild animals, unmolested, for I run through Lincoln Park Zoo near downtown Chicago. I have gotten to know them well, as charming neighbors, but I always try mentally to project the animals into their natural states.

Three rock-hopper penguins neurotically pace back and forth on a piece of concrete that has been sprayed to look like ice. I envision them free, hopping from ice floe to ice floe in Antarctica among thousands of their comic-faced cousins.

An ancient elephant stands against a wall, keeping time three ways: his body sways from side to side to one beat, his tail marks a different rhythm entirely, and his trunk moves up and down to yet a third. I struggle to imagine this sluggish giant inspiring terror in an African forest.

And the paunchy cheetah lounging on a rock shelf—could this animal belong to the species that can, on a short course, out accelerate a Porsche?

It requires a huge mental leap for me to place the penguin, the elephant, and the cheetah all back where they belong, in "the world as God sees it." Somehow, God's lesson on wildness evaporates among the moats and plastic educational placards of the zoo.

Yet, I am fortunate to live near the zoo. Otherwise, Chicago would offer up only squirrels, pigeons, cockroaches, rats, and a stray songbird. Is this what God meant when he granted Adam dominion?

It is hard to avoid a sermonic tone when writing about wild animals, for our sins against them are great indeed. The elephant population alone has decreased by eight hundred thousand in the last two decades, mostly due to poachers and rambunctious soldiers with machine guns. And every year, we destroy an area of rain forest—and all its animal residents—equal in size to the state of California.

Most wildlife writing focuses on the vanishing animals themselves, but I find myself wondering about the ultimate impact on us. What else, besides that innate appreciation for wildness, have we lost? Could distaste for authority, even a resistance to the concept of God as Lord, derive in part from an atrophied sense? God's mere mention of the animals struck a chord of awe in Job; what about us, who grow up feeding peanuts across the moat to the behemoths and leviathans?

Naturalist John Muir, who never had a vision for "the world as God sees it," reluctantly concluded, "it is a great comfort . . . that vast multitude of creatures, great and small and infinite in number, lived and had a good time of God's love before man was created."

The heavens declare the glory of God, and so do breaching whales and bouncing springboks. Fortunately, in some corners of the world, vast multitudes of creatures can still live and have a time in God's love. The least we can do is make room for them—for our sakes as well as theirs.

Philip Yancey is editor at large of Christianity Today *and co-chair of the editorial board for* Books and Culture. *Yancey's most recent book is* Prayer. *His other books include* Rumors of Another World, Reaching for the Invisible God, What's So Amazing About Grace?, Where Is God When It Hurts?, *and many others. "The God Who Can't Be Tamed" was first published in* Christianity Today, *October 1987.*

■ Open Up

Select one of these activities to launch your discussion time.

Option 1

Discuss these icebreaker questions:

- If you could be transported to any spot in the world right now to spend some time by yourself in nature, where would you want to go? The beach? The mountains? Open prairies? Why?

- Describe a time when nature inspired you to worship God. Where were you? Why did you feel that way? How did you respond to your feelings? How has your life been affected by this experience?

Option 2

Gather 'round the TV and DVD player to watch a clip from *Planet Earth*, a ground-breaking documentary series produced by the BBC/Discovery Channel. Start with the first episode, "Pole to Pole," and watch ten minutes or more together. The footage is so amazing that you may end up watching the entire thing!

(The *Planet Earth* series is available at most movie-rental stores; you can also watch video highlights of the series online at http://dsc.discovery.com/convergence/planet-earth/video-player/video-player.html)

As you watch, have pen and paper in hand and jot down adjectives or phrases that come to mind about God based on what you see. Don't evaluate what you're writing—just list any words you think of that describe God drawn from what you see in *Planet Earth*.

Afterward, discuss these questions:

• Which image or scene did you like best? Why?

• Based on what you wrote down, what does nature reveal to *you* about who God is or what God is like?

■ The Issue

Theologian and author Howard A. Snyder once wrote this in *Christianity Today*:

> Many evangelicals, especially in the United States, seem to feel that ecology is of no deep concern to God. The physical world is of little value compared to the human soul. Some ask: "Shouldn't we just stick to saving souls?"
>
> In a word, no. The question is not the motives or politics of others who are concerned about the environment, but where biblically informed and Jesus-motivated compassion leads us. We ought to do a better job of caring for the environment because "the Earth is the Lord's, and everything in it.". . . Christians ought to be the most active and effective environmentalists in America.

• Do you agree that Christians should be the most "active and effective environmentalists in America?" Explain your point of view.

• How have you seen a focus on "saving souls" contribute to a lack of concern for God's physical creation? How might our concept of God be affected by a disregard for God's creation?

■ Reflect

Take a moment to read Psalm 19:1–4, John 1:1–4, and Romans 1:20 on your own. Record your observations: Which phrases or words jump out at you? What are the key ideas in these texts? How might these texts relate to environmental issues today?

■ Let's Explore

God's presence and character can be seen in creation.

The fine-tuning of the universe is evident in the precise strengths of four basic forces. Gravity is the best known of these forces, and the weakest, with a relative strength of 1. Next comes the weak nuclear force that holds neutrons together inside an atom. It is 1,034 times stronger than gravity, but works only at subatomic distances. Electromagnetism is 1,000 times stronger than the weak nuclear force. The strong nuclear force—which keeps protons together in the nucleus of an atom—is 100 times stronger yet. If even one of these forces had a slightly different strength, the life-sustaining universe we know would be impossible.

If gravity were slightly stronger, all stars would be large, like the ones that produce iron and other heavier elements, but they would burn out too rapidly for the development of life. On the other hand, if gravity were weaker, the stars would endure, but none would produce the heavier elements necessary to form planets.

The weak nuclear force controls the decay of neutrons. If it were stronger, neutrons would decay more rapidly, and there would be nothing in the universe but hydrogen. However, if this force were weaker, all the hydrogen would turn into helium and other elements.

The electromagnetic force binds atoms to one another to form molecules. If it were either weaker or stronger, no chemical bonds would form, so no life could exist.

Finally, the strong nuclear force overcomes the electromagnetic force and allows the atomic nucleus to exist. Like the weak nuclear force, changing it would produce a universe with only hydrogen or with no hydrogen.

In sum, without planets, hydrogen, and chemical bonds, there would be no life as we know it. Besides these four factors, there are at least twenty-five others that require pinpoint precision to produce a universe that contains life. Getting each of them exactly right suggests the presence of an Intelligent Designer.[1]

- What's your response to this information? When you look at nature, what are some other examples of things that point you to a creator God?

Read Romans 1:20 together.

- Imagine you didn't have access to Scripture or were unable to attend a church. What characteristics of God could you discover simply by observing nature and learning about the created world?

Yancey highlights several passages that reveal more about how God sees the world and how he interacts with what he created. Glance through God's words to Job in Job 38:4–41:34. Read any selections from the passage that stand out to you.

- Which description of an animal or aspect of creation stood out to you most? Why?

- Yancey says that wild animals "announce to our senses the splendor of an invisible, untamable God." Think of specific wild animals highlighted in the Job passage or another animal that comes to mind for you. Which traits of God does each animal draw your attention to? Be specific and creative in your answers.

Jesus Christ is also the Creator.

When you plant a seed, its growth is a reminder of the new life Jesus brings. In fact, Jesus used that illustration in the Gospels. He is the Creator and continues to hold all things together.

Read John 1:1–4.

- In your opinion, why is it significant that Jesus was part of Creation?

- How does creation point to Christ? Can you think of examples from nature that might symbolize or point to truths about the Incarnation, salvation, redemption, grace, or forgiveness? Brainstorm together.

God's glory is declared by his creation

Read Psalm 19:1–4. (If you have time, you might also want to look at Psalm 98:4–9 and Psalm 148.)

- In what ways can we observe nature "praising" God? Brainstorm several specific examples together.

- As part of God's creation, how do you declare God's glory? In what ways is God worshipped in your everyday life?

- Imagine a beautiful work of art is destroyed by vandals. Do we similarly mar representations of God's glory when we damage God's creation? In your opinion, is this metaphor valid? Why or why not?

Yancey concludes his article by saying, "The heavens declare the glory of God, and so do breaching whales and bouncing springboks. Fortunately, in some corners of the world, vast multitudes of creatures can still live and have a time in God's love. The least we can do is make room for them—for our sakes as well as theirs."

- How is caring for creation "for our sakes"? What benefit does it have for us spiritually? How can it enrich our relationship with God?

■ Going Forward

- How has your group's discussion impacted your perspective on the natural world? How has your discussion affected your view of God and God's character?

Form pairs to read and discuss the following:

There are two sides to Allen Johnson. On the one hand, he is a conservative, evangelical Christian living in the mountains of West Virginia. On the other hand, he is an environmental activist and cofounder of Christians for the Mountains, a group of like-minded stewards that have demonstrated against coal companies and participated in Rainbow Family gatherings.

Does Allen see a contradiction between these two sides of his personality? No. In fact, he hopes that environmental stewardship will quickly become a unifying, not a dividing, issue for Christians across the nation. "God has called all of us seriously," he says, "and we should agree on one thing: to take care of his Earth."

Allen's passion for environmentalism began in 1993 while visiting Haiti with a Christian Peacemaker Team. It was there that he saw desperate farmers cutting down grapefruit trees in order to make a cash crop of charcoal. "I just started sobbing," he recalls. "It really hit me that impoverishment is so closely tied to environmental destruction."

Since that day, Johnson has been a pioneer in a growing movement called "Eco-Christianity," yet his biggest challenge has been convincing other Christians to join him in the fight instead of labeling him a "New Age wing nut" or a liberal. "My identity is not as an environmentalist," says Johnson. "It's as a Christian. Because I am Christian, I should be involved with social justice—the poor, the needy. Environmentalism is one thing in my circle, but it's not my center."

• What kind of balance did Allen Johnson find? What kind of balance do you seek on this topic?

• Review the "Do Your Part" box below. What is one idea that stands out to you as something you'd like to implement?

Spend time in prayer with your partner, praising God for specific aspects of his character as Creator.

DO YOUR PART

- Take one personal "baby step" toward creation care, such as:
  —turning your home's thermostat down (or up) one degree,
  —replacing one incandescent light bulb in your home with a compact fluorescent light bulb,
  —carpooling to work (or to your small group meeting), or
  —starting a recycle bin in your garage for your family's plastic, glass, aluminum, and paper trash.

- Go on a walk in a park or nature preserve and spend time observing the beauty of God's creation. Bring a garbage bag along with you and pick up any pieces of litter you see along the way.

- Go outside late at night (or very early in the morning) and look at the stars. As you do, quietly meditate on God's character.

- Learn about Christian organizations that are devoted to creation care, such as the Evangelical Environmental Network. Visit their Web site (www.creationcare.org) and read some of the articles.

- Plan a camping trip for your small group; make "declaring God's glory" the theme of your experience together. Include times for worship and enjoyment of nature.

How can we move beyond

debilitating skepticism and

mistrust to work toward

a biblical environmental

concern?

SCRIPTURE FOCUS	
	Genesis 2:15–17, 3:17–19
	Isaiah 11:6–9, 35:1–10
	Matthew 10:5–16
	Romans 8:18–25

ENVIRONMENTAL WAGER

■

There's a lot of doom-and-gloom language in our culture when it comes to the environment: the earth is warming, the ice caps are melting, soon islands will become submerged in rising oceans, hurricanes will swamp coastlands, and other regions will experience worsening drought. Oh, and by the way, it's *our fault*.

Some Christians have responded to claims of human-caused environmental warming with staunch disagreement. Others have turned away from environmental causes entirely (after all, those hippie tree huggers are so *weird*!). On the other hand are evangelicals who have embraced environmental causes with gusto and resolve. And somewhere in between are those who feel confused by the mixed messages from the culture and from within the church.

In his article "Environmental Wager," Andy Crouch highlights the controversy surrounding global warming while making a case for genuine environmental concern that's based on a biblical view of creation.

■ Before You Meet

Read "Environmental Wager" by Andy Crouch from *Christianity Today*.

ENVIRONMENTAL WAGER

Why evangelicals are—but shouldn't be—cool toward global warming.

by Andy Crouch

The theory is taken for granted by nearly every scientist working in the field. But because it is difficult to confirm experimentally, a few vocal skeptics continue to raise pointed questions. The skeptics find a ready audience among evangelical Christians, with groups like Focus on the Family saying that "significant disagreement exists within the scientific community regarding the validity of this theory."

I'm not talking about evolution. Or maybe I am.

The issue in question is not our distant past but our near future. The theory is the all-but-unanimous scientific consensus that human beings are changing the climate by emitting gigatons of carbon into the atmosphere, and that if we do nothing to change our behavior, the warming trend that has taken hold for the past century may well become a runaway gallop.

Prompt action could not only avert the worst consequences—extreme drought and ocean levels rising as much as three feet by 2100—but could actually open up a new era of prosperity through the development of new, more efficient technologies. Some evangelical leaders—including the editors of *Christianity Today*—have called for action to address climate change. But the Bush administration, which generally listens carefully to conservative Christians, apparently hasn't heard enough to reconsider its indifference. For many churchgoers, the issue seems murky, its complexity amplified by claims of "significant disagreement."

There is, in fact, no serious disagreement among scientists that human beings are playing a major role in global warming. The Intergovernmental Panel on Climate Change, whose scientific working group was chaired for many years by the evangelical Christian Sir John Houghton, concluded in 2001 that "most of the warming observed over the last fifty years is attributable to human activities." These conclusions, Houghton points out, were vetted by more than one hundred governments including the United States: "No assessments on any other scientific topic have been so thoroughly researched and reviewed."

Unfortunately, there is another politically loaded issue where scientific agreement has failed to convince the public. If evangelicals mistrust scientists when they make pronouncements about the future, it may be because of the history of antagonism between biblical faith and evolution. As pro-evolution philosopher Michael Ruse points out in a recent book, evolution began as an alternative to Christianity before it acquired scientific respectability. It was evolutionism—a naturalistic worldview that excluded the biblical Creator—before it was science.

The resulting battle between evolutionism and Christian faith has had countless unfortunate consequences. Some Christians resorted to a wooden interpretation of the first pages of Genesis that was no better as science than evolution was as a worldview. More recently, some scientists have reacted with fanatical hostility to the questions that proponents of Intelligent Design ask about evolution.

But perhaps no result of the creation-evolution stalemate is as potentially disastrous as the way it has stymied courageous action on climate change. In May, for a serious article about Intelligent Design that described one proponent's books as "packed with provocative ideas," the editors of *The New Yorker* chose the snippy headline, "Why intelligent design isn't." Rhetoric like that hardly disposes conservative Christians to trust the impeccably researched articles about climate change the magazine published earlier in the year.

All science is ultimately a matter of trust. The tools, methods, and mathematical skills scientists acquire over years of training are beyond the reach of the rest of us, even of scientists in different fields. Thanks to the creation-evolution debate, mistrust between scientists and conservative Christians runs deep. But those scarred by battles with evolutionists might still consider heeding the scientists who are warning us about climate change. As an evangelical scientist said to me recently, the debate over climate change is very much like Pascal's wager, that famous argument for belief in God.

Believe in God though he does not exist, Pascal argued, and you lose nothing in the end. Fail to believe when he does in fact exist, and you lose everything. Likewise, we have little to lose, and much techno-logical progress, energy security, and economic efficiency to gain, if we act on climate change now—even if the worst predictions fail to come to pass. But if we choose inaction and are mistaken, we will leave our descendants a blighted world. As Pascal said, "You must wager. It is not optional. You are embarked. Which will you choose then? Let us see."

Andy Crouch is editor of the Christian Vision Project (www.christianvisionproject. com). "Environmental Wager" was first published in Christianity Today, *August 2005, Vol. 49, No. 8, Page 66.*

■ Open Up

Select one of these activities to launch your discussion time.

Option 1

Discuss these icebreaker questions:

• When you hear the word *environmentalist*, what images or stereo-types come to mind?

• Have you ever known someone who was a die-hard environmentalist? Did he or she fit the stereotype? Explain.

• What is one environmental issue that particularly concerns you? Why?

(Here are a few ideas to spark your thinking: air and water pollution; protection of endangered species; global warming; protected lands and na-tional parks; litter; urban sprawl; the rain forests; waste/recycling; animal rights; man-made chemicals that cause health problems; factory farming.)

Option 2

If the weather permits, go on a short walk as a group and observe any forms of nature you can see around you. (Even if you are in an urban environment, you may still see dandelions in sidewalks, lovely cloudscapes, birds flying overhead, and insects; you may feel the sun or a gentle breeze.) Try to take in the many aspects of God's creation that you usually don't notice in your daily routine, look for details, listen for sounds.

After your walk, gather back together and discuss these questions:

- What did you most enjoy about focusing on nature for a brief time? Why?

- Did you observe any evidence of environmental damage during your walk? If so, what did you observe?

- When you think about future generations (or your own children), which aspects of nature do you most hope they'll be able to enjoy in years to come?

■ The Issue

In his article, Andy Crouch highlights the negative recent history between evangelicals and scientists, saying, "All science is ultimately a matter of trust. . . . Thanks to the creation-evolution debate, mistrust between scientists and conservative Christians runs deep." This mistrust, Crouch believes, has contributed to the the reluctance of many evangelicals to accept the notion of global warming.

Environmentalists are also a tough group for evangelicals to "get along" with. After all, the environmental movement includes a large number of New Agers, pantheists, Buddhists, pagans, atheists, and extremists. One such example is the environmental group VHEM (Voluntary Human Extinction Movement) whose stated belief is: "Phasing out the human race by voluntarily ceasing to breed will allow Earth's biosphere to return to good health. Crowded conditions and resource shortages will improve as we become less dense." Others in the movement believe that animals (even insects) are of equal importance as humans, that trees and rocks have a divine essence, or that Christianity is to blame for most of the world's problems (particularly environmental destruction). These few examples highlight the obvious disconnect between biblical beliefs and those of some prominent environmentalists.

Mistrust of both the scientific community and the environmental movement has led many Christians to become highly skeptical of environmental issues.

- Do you consider yourself a skeptic when it comes to environmental issues? If so, what are you most skeptical about?

- Do you feel mistrust toward the scientific community? Why or why not?

- Would you feel uncomfortable joining a cause with people whose beliefs are so starkly different from your own? Why or why not? Do you think this has affected your viewpoint on environmental issues? Explain.

■ Reflect

Take a moment to read Genesis 2:15–17, 3:17–19; Isaiah 11:6–9, 35:1–10; Matthew 10:5–16 and Romans 8:18–25 on your own. Take notes about your observations: What are the key ideas in each passage? What stands out to you most? What questions do these passages raise?

■ Let's Explore

We should approach environmental controversies with wisdom rather than reactionary skepticism.

Jesus sent his disciples out into a culture in which they were certain to face animosity, misunderstanding, distrust, and worse. Read Jesus's charge to them in Matthew 10:5–16.

- Have you ever felt like "a sheep among wolves" in our culture? Have you ever felt this type of animosity in interactions with environmentalists?

The KJV translates Matthew 10:16b this way: "be ye therefore wise as serpents, and harmless as doves."

- What do you think Jesus meant here? What might this type of wisdom and innocence look like today among those with different beliefs or ideas than our own?

When it comes to global warming, there's much disagreement within the evangelical community about how best to respond. In fact, there's a debate among evangelicals as to whether or not it's even a debatable issue!

- What do you think it looks like to be discerning, "wise as a serpent," and "innocent as a dove" when it comes to a controversial issue like global warming?

- In your opinion, what factors should influence our decision-making and what factors should not regarding global warming and other environmental issues? Explain.

Devoted and committed Christians disagree sharply on this issue. Some evangelicals are very wary of global warming; their viewpoint may be best represented by Focus on the Family in their position statement on global warming which says, in part,

> [M]any unanswered questions remain regarding global-warming claims. These include the essential matters of whether reports of increased temperatures are due to natural causes, what impact—if any—can be traced to human activity, and whether there is anything we can do to make a difference.

Other evangelicals, like Crouch, note that "There is in fact no serious disagreement among scientists that human beings are playing a major role in global warming" and wholeheartedly accept the conclusions of most scientists about humanity's role in climate change.

And yet others find a "middle ground," committing to take action while acknowleding the remaining questions and the lack of unanimity. In their recent "Southern Baptist Declaration on the Environment and Climate Change," signatories within the Southern Baptist Convention assert,

Though the claims of science are neither infallible nor unanimous, they are substantial and cannot be dismissed out of hand on either scientific or theological grounds. Therefore, in the face of intense concern and guided by the biblical principle of creation stewardship, we resolve to engage this issue without any further lingering over the basic reality of the problem or our responsibility to address it. Humans must be proactive and take responsibility for our contributions to climate change—however great or small.

- In light of your discussion about wisdom, which of the viewpoints above do you think is the most wise? Why?

Environmental problems are ultimately related to human sin.

Regardless of whether or not you think climate change is directly caused by human action or is a natural development, the Bible is clear on one thing: humankind's sin has had consequences on God's created world.

Read Genesis 2:15–17, 3:17–19 and Romans 8:18–25

- How is the evil that is resident within humankind experienced by the birds, trees, lakes, earth, etc.?

- How has sin caused creation to be in "pain"? How will creation experience release from this groaning?

- If environmental degradation is a result of the Fall—and won't ultimately be "fixed" until Christ restores it—does that let us off the hook? Should we try to take action on environmental issues such as global warming, or is it pointless? Explain your perspective.

The New Testament understanding of salvation includes recovery of creation's glory.

- What dimensions of our current existence do you think will last into eternity? What things might be so tainted with sin that they don't make the cut?

Read Isaiah 11:6–9 and 35:1–10. Here Isaiah communicates a vision of the world as God is remaking it.

- Imagine what life will be like once Jesus returns to make all things new. How will it look? How will it feel? In what way might it be different from what we experience today? What things will be the same as we know them now?

H. G. Wells wrote a powerful short story called "The Door in the Wall" about a boy who came across a green door in a white wall while playing one day. Curiosity pulled him through that door, and he found himself in a land of rich enchantment, where colors were brighter, tastes were deeper, the air was more invigorating, the animals larger and yet more accessible, and people laughed with a contented ease. Everything seemed to be more alive, more profound, more significant in that world, including play itself. When the boy left by way of the green door at the end of the day, he was never able to find the place again. But to his dying day he longed for the world on the other side of the door and never gave up his search.

- Could this be a metaphor for what Crouch writes of in his article? Might Christian investments into environmental issues rise from the taste of eternity we experience in Scripture?

- What do we know about the world that God made at the beginning of time, perfect and wonderful? What do we dream about in holy dreams of the world that God has in store for us? How do we bridge the two while living in these times? What of Eden and eternity might we begin to make real as we journey here?

■ Going Forward

In an interview on National Public Radio's *Speaking of Faith*, National Association of Evangelicals vice president of governmental affairs, Richard Cizik, said:

> The science has become so compelling that it's hard for me to believe that any Evangelical Christian is willing to say, much less a leader, as some have done, that there is no consensus on the cause, the severity, nor the solutions on the subject. I just can't believe they're willing to do that. . . . I dare say it won't be long before some of the Evangelical leaders who have said, 'Don't matter, don't care,' . . . [will] have to apologize.

- What's your reaction to Cizik's quote? Why?

At the end of his article, Crouch uses Pascal's famous wager about belief in God's existence to apply similar logic to the matter of climate change. Crouch claims that if we take action to reduce pollutants that result in climate change but it ends up that human-caused global warming was a false, we're no worse off. But "if we choose inaction and are mistaken, we will leave our descendants a blighted world."

- Do you find Crouch's argument compelling?

- Review the "Do Your Part" box below, then share with the group any actions you feel compelled to take in response to this study.

Pray together for human beings who are suffering from environmental or natural problems, such as cyclones and hurricanes or drought. Ask for God to lead you in ways you can take action on these matters.

DO YOUR PART

The ideas below are targeted toward reducing global warming. However, if you don't agree with the idea of human-caused global warming, you can still feel good about taking some of these action steps because they care for creation in other ways too by reducing pollution, energy consumption, and waste.

- Clean or replace your furnace filter. (A clean filter requires significantly less energy use and, therefore, contributes less carbon dioxide emissions.)

- When it's time to purchase a car, consider purchasing a fuel-efficient vehicle.

- Make it a habit to always turn off lights and appliances when not in use.

- Save energy by using your dryer, washing machine, and dishwasher only when they're full.

- Consider using "green" power in your house. Contact your local power utility; many have programs that enable you to use power generated from wind farms and other more eco-friendly ways.

- Plant a tree in your yard. Trees not only absorb carbon dioxide, but the shade they provide can help keep your house cooler.

Have you bought

into common myths

and prevalent

misunderstandings when it

comes to the relationship

between the church and

God's creation?

SCRIPTURE FOCUS

Psalm 8

Psalm 111

DEBUNKING ECO-MYTHS

■

Is the church to blame for the environmental crisis? After all, hasn't Christian theology regarding man's supremacy over nature been the justification for much of the environmental destruction in recent centuries?

Is it even *biblical* to be "green"? Is it appropriate to get involved in environmental causes alongside pantheists, New Agers, and anti-Christian secularists? Aren't the underpinnings of the environmental movement in direct contrast with what the Bible teaches?

Is there really any reason to try anyway? The problems are so overwhelming that it often feels like there is nothing substantial we can do. Can the church really make a significant difference?

This study will explore ideas deemed "Eco-Myths" by David Livingstone, Calvin DeWitt, and Loren Wilkinson. You'll examine together what's true—and what's false—about some of the ideas commonly held about the environment.

■ Before You Meet

Read "Eco-Myths" by David N. Livingstone, Calvin B. DeWitt, and Loren Wilkinson from *Christianity Today*.

ECO-MYTHS

Don't believe everything you hear about the
church and the environmental crisis.

by David N. Livingstone, Calvin B. DeWitt, and Loren Wilkinson

■

MYTH 1: THE CHURCH IS TO BLAME

by David N. Livingstone

In 1967, historian Lynn White, Jr., a self-professed Christian who remained a lifelong Presbyterian, provoked a furious controversy by suggesting Christianity was largely to blame for the world's environmental problems. His article in *Science* magazine "The Historical Roots of Our Ecologic Crisis" argued that Christianity had to shoulder such responsibility because its theology was hostile toward the natural order. White's article has been quoted and vigorously debated ever since.

White argued that ecological problems grew directly out of the Western world's marriage between science and technology, a marriage that gave birth to power machinery, labor-saving devices, and automation. However, he argued that the intellectual origins of this transformation actually predate both the Industrial Revolution of the late eighteenth century and the scientific revolution of the seventeenth.

He suggested that it was the medieval view of "man and nature" that brought a decisive shift in attitude: people no longer thought of themselves *as part of* nature but as having dominion *over* nature. According to White, this ruthless attitude toward nature later joined forces with a new technology to wreak environmental havoc.

White traced this exploitative attitude to the triumph of Christianity over paganism—what he called "the greatest psychic revolution in the history of our culture." Christianity, he insisted, told people that humans had a *right* to dominate nature. This contrasted with earlier religious traditions in which every tree, spring, and stream had its own guardian spirit. By eliminating animism, he wrote, "Christianity made it possible to exploit nature in a mood of indifference."

White recognized that Western Christianity encompassed a variety of distinctive theological traditions, some of which—notably that of Saint Francis of Assisi—were quite reverential toward the created order. Nevertheless, he insisted that Christianity bore "a huge burden of guilt" for the degradation of the natural world .

Since the appearance of White's article, the idea of blaming Christians for the environmental crisis has attracted a wide range of committed defenders.

The Prosecution Falters

White's arguments have also been widely criticized, of course. In 1970, historian Lewis Moncrief expressed misgivings about looking for single causes for the environmental crisis. Instead of pinning blame for environmental recklessness on Judeo-Christian dogma, he blamed a range of cultural factors. Two especially prominent were democracy and the American frontier experience. These led to affluence, changed production and consumption patterns, and problems of waste disposal. However, the absence of environmental morality, the inability of social institutions to adjust to the ecological crisis, and an abiding—if misplaced—faith in technology were the ultimate fruits.

The work of Chinese-American geographer Yi-Fu Tuan throws doubts on White's thesis in a different way. Tuan scrutinized the environmental situation in Asia and discovered that, despite its different religious traditions, *practices* there were every bit as destructive of the environment as in the West.

From a different perspective, philosopher Robin Attfield insisted that the idea that everything exists to serve humanity is not the biblical position.

God, the Wise Conservationist

As the rise of science and technology brought about profound environmental changes, Christian clergy and scientists alike outlined strategies to moderate damage to the natural habitat.

Concerned over wasteful land practices, John Evelyn (1620–1706), a founding member of the Royal Society and a Latitudinarian churchman, appealed for the institution of sound conservation practices, drew attention to agricultural encroachment on forest land, highlighted the ecological problems of unrestrained grazing, and warned of dangers from charcoal mining. His was a managerial approach to the environment. *Efficiency, production, management* were the watchwords of this pioneer conservationist.

John Graunt presented his *Natural and Political Observations Made upon the Bills of Mortality* of 1662 and argued that the orderliness of the world machine attested to the sovereignty and beneficence of its Grand Architect. Humans must exercise stewardship over the natural world to ensure that they did not efface or erase the marks of its Designer. Moreover, God was seen as a wise conservationist, and people, made in his image, were to act as caretakers of his world.

The stewardship principle had already been firmly established in John Calvin's injunction: "Let him who possesses a field, so partake of its yearly fruits, that he may not suffer the ground to be injured by his negligence; but let him endeavor to hand it down to posterity as he received it. . . . Let everyone regard himself as the steward of God in all things which he possesses."

The Beetle's "Precious" Life Before God

Cultural changes during the eighteenth and early nineteenth centuries drove people to think about their relationship to the environment even more. In response to worldwide geographical discovery, revelations about the size of the universe, and geological reports of an immensely old Earth, thinkers began more seriously to question the idea that the world existed solely for human benefit. Some argued that the human species was one more link in the chain of nature. The seeming secularism of such realizations should not blind us to the fact that it became increasingly acceptable *within* the Christian church to believe that all creatures were entitled to respect and civility.

[T]he intellectual origins of the campaign against unnecessary cruelty to animals . . . grew out of the (minority) Christian tradition that man should take care of God's creation. . . . Clerics were often ahead of lay opinion and an essential role was played by Puritans, Dissenters, Quakers, and Evangelicals.

Where Blame Is Due

To the extent that the church has failed to take concern for the environment seriously, it must accept its share of the blame. We need to cull our heritage for intellectual and spiritual resources to meet today's environmental problems.

I have concentrated on voices within the modern Western Christian tradition. There are many earlier voices as well, such as Francis of Assisi. Committed to a life of poverty and a gospel of repentance, Francis treated all living and inanimate objects as brothers and sisters and thereby insisted on the importance of communion with nature. Some believe Francis came close to heresy in his tendency to humanize the nonhuman world and have turned to other sources.

Attending to these hidden riches within the Christian heritage can do more than clear our name. They might well provide the impetus for changing worldwide environmental behavior. The scholar and theologian can and should take a vital role in addressing the current situation—and leading the church forward.

MYTH 2: IT'S NOT BIBLICAL TO BE GREEN

by Calvin B. DeWitt

I am amazed to hear Christians sometimes say that biblical faith has little in common with the environmental cause. Even worse, some evangelicals fear that teaching people to enjoy and respect creation will turn them into pantheists.

My experience has been very different. For over fifty years I have been inspired and awed by God's creation. From keeping a painted turtle in a tank at age three to caring for a backyard zoo during my youth, I gained deep appreciation for God's creatures. Because I attended a Christian school, heard two sermons every Sunday, and had parents who not only tolerated the creatures under my care but brought me up in the way I should go, there was never any question where the natural abundance around me came from. All creatures were God's—his masterpieces. They were the ones about which we sang each Sunday, "Praise God, all creatures here below!"

As a youth I savored Article II of the Reformed tradition's Belgic Confession. In answering "By What Means Is God Made Known to Us?" the first part affirms, "by the creation, preservation, and government of the universe; which is before our eyes as a most elegant book, wherein all creatures, great and small, are as so many characters leading us to see clearly the invisible things of God."

This theme of how creation tells of God's glory and love is echoed throughout Scripture: God lovingly provides the rains and cyclings of water, provides food for creatures, fills people's hearts with joy, and satisfies the earth (Ps. 104:10–18; Acts 14:17). It is through this manifest love and wisdom that creation declares God's glory and proclaims the work of the Creator's hands (Ps. 19:1). Creation gives clear evidence of God's eternal power and divinity, leaving everyone without excuse before God (Rom. 1:20).

But today we often acknowledge God as Creator without grasping what it means to be part of creation. We have alienated ourselves from the natural processes. We abuse God's creation without realizing that we thereby grieve God.

Of God's magnificent provisions in creation, I want to identify seven. These provisions, many of which are celebrated in Psalm 104, point to the beauty and integrity of what God has made. Through the ages they have led to wonder and respect for the Creator and creation. They also magnify the seriousness of our era's sometimes reckless disregard of our Father's world.

Seven Provisions of Creation

1. *Earth's energy exchange with the Sun.* Our star, the Sun, pours out immense energy in all directions, heating anything in the path of its rays. A tiny part of the Sun's energy is intercepted by our planet. This energizes everything on Earth—all life, ocean currents, the winds, and storms.

   The thin layer of gases that envelops this planet has a very important function here. This layer contains water vapor and carbon dioxide and other "greenhouse gases" that trap energy and delay some of its return to space. Earth becomes warm—but not too warm.

   The provision of these greenhouse gases—in just the right amounts—makes Earth warm enough to support the wondrous fabric of life we call the biosphere. It works very much like the glass of a greenhouse that lets sunlight in, but makes it difficult for the heat to get out. We experience this "greenhouse effect" on the sunny side of our houses and in our cars when parked in sunlight.

2. *Soil and land building.* Many of us know from gardening that soil can be made more productive through tilling and composting. This process also takes place unaided by human cultivation. Climate, rainfall, and soil organisms work together to make soils richer and more supportive of life. This entails a remarkable variety of cycles: the carbon cycle, water cycle, nitrogen cycle, and so on. This symphony of processes enables even bare rock eventually to support a rich fabric of living things. What a remarkable provision! It nurtures the fruitfulness of creation.

3. *Cycling, recycling, and ecosystems.* Recycling is not a recent invention. The whole creation uses and reuses substances contained in soil, water, and air. Carbon dioxide breathed out by us—and raccoons, lizards, and gnats—enters the atmosphere later to be taken up as the carbon-based raw material from which to make the carbon-based stuff of life. This is in turn transferred to the animals and microscopic life that depend upon it for food. And soon these consuming creatures return the carbon back to the atmosphere through breathing, or by their own death and decay.

Water, too, is recycled. Taken up by animals, it is released through breathing, sweating, and ridding of wastes—finding its way into the atmosphere, or through sewage-treatment plants back to rivers and streams. Taken up by the roots of plants, some is pumped up through the bundles of tubing in the roots, stems, and leaves of plants and back to the atmosphere. That moisture joins water evaporated from lakes, streams, and other surfaces and forms rain and snow that again water the face of Earth.

Thinking of such provision, the psalmist wrote,

> He makes springs pour water into the ravines; it flows between the mountains. They give water to all the beasts of the field; the wild donkeys quench their thirst. . . . He waters the mountains from his upper chambers; the earth is satisfied by the fruit of his work. (Ps. 104:10–13; NIV)

4. *Water purification.* Some water percolates through the soil to the ground water below and supplies the springs that feed wetlands, lakes, and ravines; we call this percolation. In many water-treatment plants in our cities, water is purified by having it percolate through beds of sand. In similar fashion, water that percolates through soil or rock is filtered, but usually over much greater distances. The result: by the time we pull up water to our homes by our wells, it usually is fit to drink.

5. *Fruitfulness and abundant life.* Of the known flowering plants alone, there are 250,000 species . . . And each of these interrelates with water, soil, air, and other organisms, forming the interwoven threads of the household of life we call the biosphere. When I was in ninth grade, I recall learning that there were 1 million different species of living creatures. In graduate school, I learned that it was 5 million, and today we believe it is somewhere between 5 million and 40 million. This biodiversity is so great that we have just begun to name the creatures. This is just the kind of provision you would expect from a remarkably creative Genius. "The earth is full of your creatures," said the psalmist. "There is the sea, vast and spacious, teeming with creatures beyond number" (Ps. 104:24–25, NIV).

6. *Global circulations of water and air.* Because of its 23.5-degree tilt, our Earth gets unequally heated from season to season. Both seasonal and daily differences cause differentials in Earth's temperatures. This, in turn, produces temperature gradients that drive the flow of water and air from place to place.

Atmospheric and oceanic circulations are vital provisions for maintaining life. Carbon dioxide produced by animal and plant respiration and oxygen produced by photosynthesis are released to air and water. Carbon dioxide is moved around so that it comes into contact with plants that reincorporate it. And oxygen, produced by photosynthesis of plants, is similarly circulated by air and water currents. Global circulations provide the "breath" of life on a planetary scale.

7. *Human ability to learn from creation.* Human beings are endowed by God with minds that integrate what creation teaches us. Through observation and experiment, we are able to revise our models of the world to represent reality better. Our mental models are further nurtured and refined by the cultures we grow up in. This capability is essential for meaningful human life.

Seven Degradations

Human beings can mute and diminish God's testimony in creation. We have the ability, in the words of Revelation 11:18, to "destroy the earth." Nearly every day now, we learn about new destructions of land and creatures. While some reports are dramatized and overstated, professional technical literature again and again describes new and increasing instances of environmental degradation. What I present here as "seven degradations" draws upon scholarly literature accepted by the scientific community. That means I have not gotten my information from government or university reports, newspapers, opinion polls, television, talk shows, or popular articles. Practically every one of these degradations is a destruction of one of God's provisions for creation.

1. *Land conversion and habitat destruction.* Since 1850, people have converted 2.2 billion acres of natural lands to human use. This compares with Earth's total of 16 billion acres that have some kind of vegetation and current world crop land of 3.6 billion acres. This conversion of land

goes by different names: deforestation (forests), drainage or "reclamation" (wetlands), irrigation (arid and semiarid ecosystems), and opening (grasslands and prairies). The greatest conversion under way is tropical deforestation, which removes about 25 million acres of primary forest each year . . . The immensity of this destruction illustrates our new power to alter the face of Earth.

2. *Species extinction.* More than three species of plants and animals are extinguished daily. If there are indeed 40 million species, then the rate may be several times higher.

3. *Land degradation.* What once was tall-grass prairie we now call the Corn Belt; here we grow the corn that feeds hogs, cattle, and us. In much of this prairie, two bushels of topsoil are lost for every bushel of corn produced. Pesticides and herbicides made it possible to plant corn, or any crop, year after year on the same land. Crop rotation—from corn to soy beans to alfalfa hay to pastures—has been abandoned.

4. *Resource conversion and wastes and hazards production.* Some seventy thousand chemicals have been created by our ingenuity. Unlike chemicals made by organisms and the earth, some cannot be absorbed back into the environment. Among them are many specifically designed to destroy life: biocides, pesticides, herbicides, avicides, and fungicides.

5. *Global toxification.* Of the thousands of chemical substances we have created, hundreds have been discharged or have leaked into the atmosphere, rivers, and ground water. This happens through "disposal" and from vehicles, chemical agriculture, homes, and industry. Some join global circulations. DDT has shown up in Antarctic penguins, and biocides appear in a remote lake on Lake Superior's Isle Royale. Cancer has become pervasive in some herring gull populations.

6. *Alteration of planetary exchange.* Earth's exchange of energy with the Sun and outer space is fundamental to the planet's circulations of air and water. But burning and exposing carbon-containing materials to oxygen brings rising concentrations of atmospheric carbon dioxide,

allowing less heat to escape to outer space, thereby enhancing the greenhouse effect. This creates global warming.

7. *Human and cultural degradation.* One of the most severe reductions of creation's richness concerns cultures that have lived peaceably on the land for centuries. In the tropics, cultures living cooperatively with the forest are being wiped off the land by coercion, killing, and legal procedures that deprive them of traditional lands. Their rich heritage of unwritten knowledge is being lost.

A Place for Evangelicals?

The evangelical community has been slow to get involved in environmental issues. But it is not too late. In the early 1970s there were few evangelicals involved in world hunger. Today some of the best relief operations are done by these deliberative evangelicals. They did not just start handing out food. They got the best minds together, collected the scriptural material, and carefully planned.

That needs to happen again. Our environmental situation presents a significant opportunity. To be *evangelical* means to proclaim the good news. Part of our proclamation is that the environment is God's *creation.* If we do not make God the Creator part of the good news, we are crippling our faith and witness. We will lose sight of what the Belgic Confession called "a most elegant book" wherein all creatures help us—and others— to see the invisible God.

MYTH 3: THERE IS NOTHING CHRISTIANS CAN DO

by Loren Wilkinson

Headlines trumpet news of environmental crises, with some experts claiming apocalyptic scenarios where we will either burn or freeze within a generation. Another vociferous group claims just the opposite: there is no real ecological problem, only hysterical environmentalists. Despite their divergent messages, both groups offer Christians the same temptation: to think there is nothing we can do to help the situation.

But this is simply not true. There are many strategies Christians can and should pursue to help care for creation.

One of the earliest evangelical books on the environment—Francis Schaeffer's *Pollution and the Death of Man*—made one of the wisest observations: Christian households and churches need to be "pilot plants" of the new creation. There the world can see, acted out in individual lives and in communities, the healing of creation that only comes from being in fellowship with God in Christ. Eugene Peterson's rendering of Philippians 2:15 suggests the difference we can make: "Go into the world uncorrupted, a breath of fresh air in this squalid and polluted society. Provide people with a glimpse of good living and of the living God" (*The Message*).

What does "good living and the living God" mean when it comes to creation? What can we do? Here are some suggestions, organized in ever-widening spheres of influence:

Individual Action

First, we become *aware*. We learn how God cares and provides for us through creation. That means, for example, knowing where our food, water, and energy come from and where our waste products go. This is not to reduce us to guilty inaction, but to make us know that it is through God's creation that we live.

We also need to practice the principles of "reduce, reuse, recycle"— not out of environmentalist legalism but in conscious delight of being God's free, redeemed, and responsible stewards.

We *reduce*, for example, because, though creation is for our use, it has worth far beyond the use we make of it. The more we learn the impact of our choices on creation, the more likely we are to learn to be content with less.

We *reuse* because God did not make a throwaway world. So repair the shoes or toaster to give them new or longer life. If we must bring things home in packaging, we ought to consider the second life the packages might have. And we ought to be willing to pay more for things that have a longer life.

And we *recycle* because God does. "To the place the streams come from, there they return again," says Psalm 104. Increasingly, however, we have built a civilization whose residues—plastics, tires, Styrofoam—do not fit into the created cycles. So when we must discard what we have used, we need to recycle.

To these three R's, Christians have good reason to add two more:

We *resist*. Our culture often defines our value in terms of how much we consume. We need to resist this consumerism that is fed by advertising and television. In few other areas can we better demonstrate "good living" and our allegiance to "the living God" than by refusing to be shaped by our consumerist culture.

But that negative choice opens up a glorious, positive one: We *rejoice*. The more we learn about God's provisions for the earth, the more wonderful it seems. Isaiah's words should describe our experience of creation: "You will go out in joy and be led forth in peace; the mountains and the hills will burst into song before you, and all the trees of the field will clap their hands" (Isa. 55:12 NIV).

Community Efforts

We should get in the habit of using the theological term *creation* instead of the more secular *environment* or *nature*. The bedrock of our action is that we are *creatures*, responsible to God our Creator for our use of his gifts in creation. A congregation that speaks only of "the environment" may well come to feel that its wastebaskets full of plastic foam cups on Sunday morning offend only some politically correct fad.

We also need to broaden our understanding of the word *stewardship*. Inside the church the term is restricted almost entirely to matters of money. But increasingly it is being used outside the church to speak of our care of creation. The word opens a door to witness, for it invites the question, "To *whom* is the steward responsible?"

If the church is to be a model of "good living and the living God," we also need to be aware of what our buildings and practices convey about God and the genuinely good life. All the principles of caring for creation that we practice as individuals—reducing, reusing, recycling, resisting, and rejoicing—should be evident in our corporate life as well. Ultimately, to a pagan world beginning to glimpse something of God through creation, these acts function as pre-evangelism.

Church members should also consider reducing their impact on creation through sharing. Many things that we own—from lawn mowers to vacation homes—could well be shared.

Finally, churches should resist an increasing tendency to leave God's creative acts out of worship. Much new worship music exalts God in his majesty but speaks very little of what he has done and made.

Public Witness

Christians have recently begun to be more aware of their need to be politically active. We need to extend that activity to policies that influence our care of creation. It is important to shape the way our governments and economies work. We need to bring the full meaning of words like *creation* and *stewardship* into the public arena. Here are four principles for wider involvement.

1. Many of the most important political decisions related to the care of creation are influenced greatly by opinions of local people. Zoning hearings to increase the density of an area, or to allow roads, industry, or power plants, invite public participation. It is important to use such forums in order to save our communities, and to do so publicly in the name of God the Creator.

2. Just as we have (rightly) evaluated candidates for office on their records on such issues as abortion and attitude toward the family, we need to evaluate also their attitudes toward creation.

3. A major problem in our civilization is the barrier between cities and the agriculture that supports them. (The average food item in North America is transported more than eight hundred miles.) This leads to ever-larger farms and ever-fewer opportunities for stewardship and contact with the creation that supports us.

4. Some of the most eloquent and effective voices for the care of creation come from environmental groups in which there is no Christian presence (and often an implicitly anti-Christian bias). Christians should consider participating in such groups, both because their agenda—caring for creation—should be a Christian's agenda, and because these organizations desperately need a Christian witness.

> The environmental movement is an ethic looking for a religion, and it is no surprise that many people in it have turned to native and pagan religions when no Christian voice speaks with and to them.

"Eco-Myths" was first published online at www.christianitytoday.com in June 2001. David N. Livingstone is a professor in the School of GeoSciences at the Queen's University of Belfast. He is the author of Darwin's Forgotten Defenders *(Eerdmans) and* The Geographical Tradition *(Blackwell). Calvin B. DeWitt is an environmental scientist with the Institute for Environmental Studies at the University of Wisconsin-Madison and director of the AuSable Institute of Environmental Studies, a Christian center for the integration of biblical teaching and environmental science for college students, professors, and churches. He is the author of* Earth-Wise *(CRC) and the general editor of* The Environment and the Christian *(Baker). Loren Wilkinson is the coauthor, with his wife, Mary Ruth Wilkinson, of* Caring for Creation in Your Own Backyard *(Servant). He teaches at Regent College in Vancouver, British Columbia.*

■ Open Up

Select one of these activities to launch your discussion time.

Option 1

Discuss these icebreaker questions:

- Were you surprised by any of the eco-myths proposed by the authors? Explain.

- Do you think it's a sin to throw away an aluminum can rather than recycle it? Why or why not?

Consider the many different ways Christians respond to environmental issues. On one end of the spectrum are people who are staunchly "against" efforts to care for creation and who consider environmental causes to be weird or unbiblical. On the other end are people who have made creation care their life's greatest passion.

Against environmental care or action	Passionate about creation care

- Where would you place yourself on this spectrum? Why?

Option 2

Write each of the following statements on its own piece of poster board—or chalkboard to be even more eco-friendly:

There is nothing in the Bible about creation care.
Caring for the earth means worshiping the earth, not God.
Global warming is an act of God, not a cause of human impact.
Christians should be concerned about people and not the planet.
If you support creation care, you must be a Democrat.

You may think these statements are completely false; you may see a kernel of truth in each of them; or you may generally agree with each of them. Your challenge: work together as a group to re-organize the posters into order that your group can agree upon, ranging from "least true" to "most true." When you're done, talk about this question:

- Do you personally think these statements are eco-myths? If so, which ones are? Or which statements do you agree with?

From your experience, which of these viewpoints are most common within the church? Work together to reorganize the posters again by grouping the "least common" and "most common" ideas together. Talk about your encounters with people who have the opinions represented on these cards, then discuss:

- Step inside the mind-set of people who hold these opinions. Why do you think they feel that way? Explain the rationale—whether you personally agree with it or not.

As a group, brainstorm and add some additional common eco-myths posters to your collection. Keep the posters in the front of your room so you can reference them during your study and discussion. (Recycle them when you're finished!)

■ The Issue

Read these statements from two different evangelical Christian organizations:

We believe the harm caused by mandated reductions in energy consumption in the quixotic quest to reduce global warming will far exceed its benefits. Reducing energy consumption will require significantly increasing the costs of energy—whether through taxation or by restricting supplies. Because energy is a vital component in producing all goods and services people need, raising its costs means raising other prices too. For wealthy people, this might require some adjustments in consumption patterns— inconvenient and disappointing, perhaps, but not devastating. But for the world's 2 billion or more poor people, who can barely afford sufficient food, clothing, and shelter to sustain life, and who are without electricity and the refrigeration, cooking, light, heat, and air conditioning it can provide, it can mean the difference between life and death.

From the Cornwall Alliance for the Stewardship of Creation, "An Open Letter to the Signers of 'Climate Change: An Evangelical Call to Action' and Other Concerns About Global Warming" (http://www.cornwallalliance.org).

Even small rises in global temperatures will have such likely impacts as: sea level rise; more frequent heat waves, droughts, and extreme weather events such as torrential rains and floods; increased tropical diseases in now-temperate regions; and hurricanes that are more intense . . . It could lead to significant reduction in agricultural output, especially in poor countries . . . Poor nations and poor individuals have fewer resources available to cope with major challenges and threats. The consequences of global warming will therefore hit the poor the hardest, in part because those areas likely to be significantly affected first are in the poorest regions of the world. Millions of people could die in this century because of climate change, most of them our poorest global neighbors.

From the Evangelical Climate Initiative, "Climate Change: An Evangelical Call to Action" (http://www.christiansandclimate.org/).

Discuss these questions:

• Do you think either one of these statements is an eco-myth? Why or why not?

• Do you think these statements contradict each other? Why or why not?

■ Reflect

As individuals spend time with these Scriptures, consider quietly playing a worship song such as "God of Wonders" or "Shout to the Lord."

Take a moment to read Psalm 8 and 111 on your own. Take notes about your observations. What words, phrases, or images jump out to you? Which of your own encounters with nature come to mind as you read? What do you discover about God and God's character in these passages?

■ Let's Explore

Creation care has historically been integral to the church.

In his exploration of Myth #1 in "Eco-Myths," David N. Livingstone writes about Lynn White, who claimed in 1967 that the degradation of God's creation has a direct correlation to the growth of Christianity and that the relationship between man and nature shifted as a result of Christian ideas.

- Read Psalm 8. How does the Psalmist view man's relationship with God's creation? How is this like or unlike the way Christians today think about our relationship with the created world?

- Do you think people today see themselves as the "rulers" or "in charge of" the world God created (Psalm 8:6)? What types of responsibility come with that role? Discuss what you think this role should involve.

Livingstone suggests that Christians actually posed objections to the degradation caused more directly by advances in science and technology. Very early in the life of the church, theologians were advocating that humans "must exercise stewardship over the natural world to ensure that they did not efface or erase the marks of its Designer."

- In what ways are Christians today in danger of "erasing the marks of our Designer?"

God's good provision is evident in the created world.

Often Christians feel that they have to justify their love for animals or nature because the environmental movement has a motive that's counter-Christian. Cal DeWitt notes that we often "acknowledge God as Creator without grasping what it means to be part of creation."

DeWitt is not alone in asserting that it is indeed *very* biblical to be "green." In his book *The Birds, Our Teachers,* pastor (and birdwatcher) John Stott wrote, "Since 'the works of the Lord' (Psalm 111:2 NRSV) refer to his works of both creation and redemption, it seems to me that nature study and Bible study should go together. Many Christians have a good doctrine of redemption, but need a better doctrine of creation."

- Do you agree that "nature study and Bible study should go together"? Explain, sharing from your own experiences.

- Describe your awareness of the seven magnificent provisions in creation DeWitt explores. Which stands out to you most? Why?

- Read Psalm 111. Which provisions of God does the psalmist highlight? If you could add a line or two to this psalm, what other provisions of God in the created world would you want to mention?

- Describe your awareness of the seven degradations of those provisions that DeWitt outlines. How have you disregarded or participated in one of them? What does that disregard do to the relationship we have with God? Explain which one of those degradations might have the most serious affect on our relationship with God and why.

- In light of what you've read in Psalm 8 and Psalm 111, do you think the psalmist is an "environmentalist"? Why or why not?

We each must take action in response to environmental degradations.

Loren Wilkinson cites three different types of action Christians should take in regard to creation care: individual, community effort, and public witness.

- Which type of action do you feel most comfortable with? Which do you think is the greatest challenge for the church today?

- Have you ever felt called by God to be a voice for God's creation? Has anything stopped you previously from doing so? Explain.

- What kinds of actions or choices do you imagine the psalmists might have been taking to care for creation in the name of God? How would these psalms be different if they were written by someone who was simply admiring natural wonders?

- What does Psalm 8 say about our responsibility to God and his creation? How does the type of action that Loren Wilkinson describes fit in with our calling as stewards of the natural world?

■ Going Forward

Form pairs for this final portion of the study.
The "Eco-Myths" article highlights these three erroneous ideas:

1. The church is to blame.
2. It's not biblical to be green.
3. There is nothing Christians can do.

• Before your group's discussion, which of these myths did you accept or relate to? How has your perspective changed?

• Imagine a conversation with someone in your family or from your church who believes one of these myths. What would you say to help him or her develop a more informed perspective?

Review the "Do Your Part" box below, and tell your partner one action step you plan to take. Then pray for each other and your efforts to care for God's creation.

DO YOUR PART

Here are four ideas for each of the 4 Rs highlighted by Loren Wilkinson.

Reduce: Reduce usage of environmentally harmful plastic bags at grocery stores by bringing your own bags.

Reuse: Instead of throwing them out, reuse plastic containers, glass bottles, and jars. Thoroughly wash them, then use them to store leftovers, cooking oil, or knick-knacks.

Recycle: In additional to recycling paper, plastic, and aluminum via your local recycling service, recycle "garbage" like carrot peelings or leftover lettuce to create compost to fertilize your garden.

Resist: Resist the influence of our consumerism-driven culture by "fasting" from shopping for a week (or perhaps a month). Determine what your necessities are and buy *only* those things you truly need.

What does God expect of us

as stewards of his world?

SCRIPTURE FOCUS

Genesis 1:26–30, 2:15

Psalm 104

Luke 19:11–27

CREATION'S

CARETAKERS

■

God cares about unborn babies—and so should we. God also cares about bald eagles? So, should we? And if so, *how much*?

In his article "Conservation: Protecting Bald Eagles and Babies," John Silvius expands on that point, calling for Christians to embrace and embody a lifestyle of "compassionate conservationism." In this study you'll wrestle with issues of stewardship and conservation as you consider what it means to be the "rulers" God has placed over the earth.

■ Before You Meet

Read "Conservation: Protecting Bald Eagles and Babies" by John E. Silvius from *Christianity Today*.

CONSERVATION: PROTECTING BALD EAGLES AND BABIES

The case for compassionate conservationism

by John E. Silvius

Limited energy supply and impending higher fuel prices emerged as early tests of George W. Bush's leadership. His proposal to increase energy supplies by extracting oil from the Alaska National Wildlife Refuge angered many who want to preserve this beautiful natural area. These plans and Bush's withdrawal of US support for the Kyoto Accord, which would limit emissions of greenhouse gases, didn't surprise environmentalists, who opposed his election because of what they considered his disregard for the environment. Indeed, political or economic conservatives generally have difficulty gaining the confidence and support of environmentalists, even if conservatives propose resource extraction in an "environmentally friendly manner."

Many moral conservatives believe the philosophies of free market and limited government have a biblical basis. At the same time, these philosophies have led many industries to act irresponsibly, resulting in unnecessary destruction of landscapes, habitats, water, and air. The problem, however, is not conservative politics and economics *per se*. Rather, the problem is the conservatives' failure to articulate and implement an environmental ethic that controls human behavior.

Moral conservatives are successfully articulating a biblical worldview regarding sexual abstinence before marriage, sanctity of life, and the importance of moral teaching in our schools. Consistent with this, they must also articulate the case for a compassionate conservationism, an environmental ethic rooted in a biblical worldview. Such an ethic would redefine *environmentalists* as "those who are concerned about the environment of *all of life*." Thus they would care about the environment of the bald eagle chick, especially when the egg crushes under the weight of the mother because the eggshell has been weakened by pesticides in the food chain. But they would also seek protection of the unborn baby from all threats, whether they be humanly introduced toxins and abortifacients or environmental pollutants that the baby might encounter through the mother.

A compassionate conservationist would listen carefully to the environmentalist concerned for bald eagles and their habitats, but would also explain that the Creator of heaven and earth is not only concerned for every sparrow that falls (Matt. 10:29) but also every unborn baby: He sees even in the womb (Ps. 139).

Does compassionate conservationism extend to the point of giving "equal rights" to human and nonhuman creatures alike? Genesis says that God gave humans "dominion" over the created world (1:28). This dominion is not license to abuse animals and animals' habitats but is characterized by "tilling" (or serving) and "keeping" (or preserving the ongoing fruitfulness of) the Earth (2:15). Here, we discover the biblical roots of true conservationism: as we serve creation, creation serves us (i.e. *con*servation, or "serving with" creation).

Sin in the garden (Gen. 3)—human rejection of God's authority and abuse of the fruit of the garden—led to God's judgment. But the responsibility of stewardship remains and can be exercised only by people with servant hearts who recognize that God is the owner and that we are the keepers of creation. People who live as God's stewards find fulfillment in their Creator and are released from the grip of materialism that for too long has left its footprints on scarred landscapes carelessly ravaged to support the wants and needs of humans whose god is this world. Responsible stewards are freed from endless anxiety and arguments about whether we are running out of resources. Instead, they work to please the Creator by proper stewardship of resources out of love and faithfulness to God. They practice compassionate conservation.

With enlightened support of citizens who understand and practice compassionate conservation, our president and other national, state, and local officials can lead in developing environmental policies that are consistent and comprehensive. Such policies would respect both the habitats of God's creatures and the resource needs of people, because the policies emphasize true stewardship of what belongs not to us but to God. They promote respect and concern for all environments in creation—the habitats of creatures, the environment of our homes and schools, and even the cradle of life, the environment of the womb.

John E. Silvius is professor of biology at Cedarville (Ohio) University and author of Biology: Principles and Perspectives. *"Conservation: Protecting Bald Eagles and Babies" first appeared in* Christianity Today *on June 11, 2001, Vol. 45, No. 8.*

■ Open Up

Select one of these activities to launch your discussion time.

Option 1

Discuss these icebreaker questions:

- What is the most important material object you've ever been entrusted with or been asked to care for?

- What is your most treasured possession? Why is it meaningful to you?

- Other than a family member, who would you choose to take care of that object in your absence? Why?

Option 2

Take a moment to each individually consider this question: *Which possession that you've brought with you to the meeting is the most valuable to you?* This could be something on your person (such as an article of clothing, favorite shoes, or special earrings); items in your purse or wallet; or anything else you've brought with you.

Once you've decided which item is most valuable to you, have "Show and Tell" time as a group. Tell each other what you selected and why it's more valuable to you than the other items you've brought with you or that you're wearing.

When you're done, discuss:

- Now think about things that are truly valuable to you—such as your house or a family heirloom. Who would you trust to take care of those items in your absence? Why?

■ The Issue

- When and how is stewardship usually discussed at your church or among Christians you know? How do you think most Christians would generally define stewardship?

- How is stewardship regarding money like or unlike environmental stewardship?

■ Reflect

Take a moment to read Genesis 1:26–30, 2:15; Psalm 104; and Luke 19:11–27 on your own. Write down any words, phrases, or questions that stand out to you. Take note of key ideas and issues you observe in each passage.

■ Let's Explore

God cares for all living things.

Read Psalm 104 aloud, taking turns so that all group members can read some.

• Based on this psalm, what is God like? How would you characterize God's relationship with creation? In the psalm's figurative language, how do created things regard God?

Jesus also emphasized the way God cares for creation, reminding listeners that the Heavenly Father feeds the birds (Matt. 6:26) and God does not forget a single sparrow (Luke 12:6).

• What specific examples from Psalm 104 point out ways God cares for creation? What other examples of God's care for creation would you add?

• Think of some of your most treasured possessions, such as a family heirloom, a car, or a piece of artwork. Or how about care for family members or pets? What practical things do you do to care for these possessions, creatures, or people?

- How is the care you take of special possession or loved ones like or unlike God's care for the created world?

God charged humans with caring for creation

Read Genesis 1:26–30 together. Here God very clearly sets humankind above animals and other created beings. But the meaning of this passage—and its implications in humanity's relationship with the rest of creation—have varied widely throughout human history.

- Some Bible translations render "rule" as "have dominion over." What are some of the different ways this idea of rule and dominion could be understood or interpreted? Share any examples from history or from people you know who hold varying viewpoints on this relationship between humanity and the rest of the created world.

Read Genesis 2:15. In his article Silvius points out how this verse can inform one's understanding of what "dominion" or "rule" means in Genesis 1. He wrote,

> Genesis says that God gave humans "dominion" over the created world (1:28). This dominion is not license to abuse animals and animals' habitats but is characterized by "tilling" (or serving) and "keeping" (or preserving the ongoing fruitfulness of) the Earth (2:15). Here, we discover the biblical roots of true conservationism: as we serve creation, creation serves us (i.e. *con*servation, or "serving with" creation).

Another important cue for God's intention in creating humankind to rule over the created world is found in Genesis 1:27.

- If humans are created in God's image—meant to reflect God's character—what should humanity's "rule" of nature be like? What kind of ruler is God? Which of God's traits do you think we should most strive to emulate in our care of creation?

- When it comes to caring for creation, what do you think is God's job? What is our job?

We should live as trustworthy stewards.

Psalm 24:1 declares, "The earth belongs to the LORD, and everything in it." In Leviticus God reminds his people of this truth. Read Leviticus 25:23–24.

The NIV translates God's words in verse 23 as, "you are but aliens and *my tenants*" (italics added).

- When have you been a tenant (such as living in an apartment)? How might your thinking about environmental issues change if you were to consider yourself as a tenant who will give an accounting to the landlord (God) for your care of his place?

Read Jesus's parable in Luke 19:11–27.

- This parable is often cited in regard to spiritual gifts. But taking a more broad interpretation, what does it say about stewardship? What principles or ideas do you think Jesus is aiming to get across to his audience?

Jesus reiterates his point about higher expectations placed on those who're given responsibility for important things several times. If you have time, also read Luke 12:48 and 16:10.

Steward is a term we don't often use in contemporary English. The word comes from the Old English *stigweard* which literally meant "hall guard." *Stigweard* was used to describe someone whose job was both to guard and care for his master's home. Synonyms for *steward* include: administrator, caretaker, conservator, custodian, guardian, manager, and watchman.

- Based on what you've read and discussed, how would you define what it means to be a "good steward" when it comes to the environment?

Examples of humankind's poor stewardship of the world God has entrusted to us to care for abound, but let's zero in on just one: our treatment of animals and other living things. Various species of plants, insects, and animals, which God created, are becoming extinct at alarming rates due to destruction of habitat and other human-caused environmental changes. Some scientific estimates conclude that around thirty-five—and possibly up to 150—species become extinct *every day*. Even the most conservative estimates (about three species per day) reveal a pretty awful track record!

• Did you realize this was happening? What's your reaction to these sta-
tistics? In what ways could you personally influence this issue?

■ Going Forward

Form pairs to discuss these next two questions.
Read the following quote from John Silvius's article:

[T]he responsibility of stewardship remains and can be exercised only by
people with servant hearts who recognize that God is the owner and that
we are the keepers of creation. . . . [T]hey work to please the Creator by
proper stewardship of resources out of love and faithfulness to God. They
practice compassionate conservation.

• If God as the "owner" of planet Earth asked you, a tenant and steward,
to give an accounting for what you have (or haven't) done to care for it,
what would you say? What issues come to mind for you as you consider
this question?

• How do you personally want to be more like God in the way you "rule"
the living beings and resources on this planet?

Pray with your partner about your desire to live as a trustworthy steward who reflects God's character in the way you care for creation.

DO YOUR PART

Here are several things you can do to practice stewardship through wildlife conservation:

- Learn more about threatened animal species by taking at least fifteen minutes to peruse ARKive's photographs and video images of threatened species. Go to http://www.arkive.org/species/GES/ and select the various animals you'd like to learn about.

- Research endangered species that are native to your area. Learn about their habitat and what specific causes are threatening their survival in your region. You can find out more at http://www.fws.gov/Endangered/wildlife.html.

- Support organizations that seek to protect the plants and animals God created, such as the National Wildlife Federation. Subscribe to a magazine or purchase a calendar or book. (NWF creates great children's magazines, including *Your Big Backyard* and *Ranger Rick*.) Go to www.nwf.org for more information.

- One of the most significant causes of species endangerment and extinction right now is destruction of the rainforests. Rainforests are cut down for a variety of reasons, including production of paper and wood and clearing of grazing land for beef cattle. Do your part to lesson demands for such items by purchasing paper and toiletries made from recycled materials and eating less beef.

- Contact a nearby botanical garden or horticulture group and learn about the plants, trees, and shrubs that are native to your area; also find out which non-native plants are considered invasive and are threatening the survival and flourishing of plants native to your region. If you have non-native invasive plants in your yard, replace them with some native wildflowers or shrubs. (You can learn more at Web sites like www.enature.com or www.plantnative.org.)

What does environmentalism have to do with loving your neighbor?

SCRIPTURE FOCUS

Psalm 104:10–31

Isaiah 1:15–17

Matthew 22:34–40

ON EARTH . . .

AS IT IS IN HEAVEN

■

What is our reaction when we hear about one person raising a hand to inflict harm to another person? We are upset . . . frightened . . . sad . . . angry.

What is our reaction when the harm is done, not just to one person, but to an entire community? When children are the ones hurt the most? We point to scriptures that condemn violence, and we call for swift and meaningful justice.

What is our reaction when the harm is perpetuated not through a hand or other violent means but through environmental degradation?

Using Hunter Farrell's article, we'll consider our response to environmental degradation that affects our most vulnerable neighbors.

■ Before You Meet

Read Hunter Farrell's *Christianity Today* article titled "Cleaning Up La Oroya."

CLEANING UP LA OROYA

How American and Peruvian Christians teamed up when factory pollutants were poisoning children.

by Hunter Farrell

Something's very wrong here," said Esther Hinostroza. "It's the children." Hinostroza was calling from her Peruvian town of La Oroya, speaking with members of the Joining Hands Network of Peru. The group is composed of fifteen Peruvian evangelical churches and Christian nonprofits and nineteen Presbyterian congregations in Missouri, Illinois, and Ohio, who together seek to bring aid and development to Peru's poor. We welcomed Hinostroza's plea, but our organization was only two years old. The network wasn't prepared to take on an international corporation, whose factory, we would discover, was polluting the town, causing the children of La Oroya to become seriously ill.

Hinostroza is a women's leader in the evangelical church of Peru, as well as director of a small nonprofit group that focuses on maternal-child health issues in the city of La Oroya. She called the network in January 2002, begging members to see firsthand some of the children's health problems. The children complained of headaches, difficulty concentrating in school, and fatigue. Members of Joining Hands agreed to come see for themselves.

La Oroya is home to a large metal ore smelter, owned by the Doe Run Company of St. Louis. When members of Joining Hands arrived and traveled with Hinostroza to the village, they were shocked. The antiquated smelter emits more than one thousand tons of toxic emissions each day. Employees say nothing about the pollution for fear of losing their jobs. Often, the city's children cannot play outdoors because of the smelter's emissions.

Pastors from the network met a seven-year-old boy named Javier; he complained of intense headaches, lethargy, and problems in school. His parents worried that the city's heavy metal contamination caused a growing curvature on his skull. Javier's experience served to focus the prayers and action of Joining Hands in the coming months. "Our children would be like Javier if we lived here," gasped one pastor after the initial visit in 2002.

Hinostroza and other Christians in La Oroya wanted to find out the extent of the city's pollution and the damage to their children's health. But they didn't have the money or know-how to conduct a scientific study. Besides, it was far beyond the scope of what Hinostroza expected of her ministry. "We were accustomed to giving hungry people a fish in Christ's name and even teaching them to fish," said Hinostroza. "But we had never given thought to what Jesus would have done when the river which runs through their town is contaminated."

The Pharmacist, the Pastor, and the Archbishop

In order to fix the problems in La Oroya, Hinostroza would need the help of Christians outside those she normally dealt with. In July 2002, Joining Hands called upon Patty Nussle, a pharmacist in the poison control unit at Children's Hospital in Columbus, Ohio, and an active member of a Joining Hands congregation. Nussle and a team from her church provided lead testing to more than sixty children.

While their sampling was not representative of the community, the test results were off the charts. "As the lab results were coming in that day in La Oroya," Nussle recalled, "I could see that almost every child was severely lead poisoned." Some children had more than six times the World Health Organization maximum permissible level, a severity of lead poisoning that in the United States requires immediate hospitalization. Before she left La Oroya, Nussle made sure Hinostroza and other mothers in La Oroya knew what even mild lead poisoning could do to children and expectant mothers: reduce a child's intelligence, stunt physical growth, cause behavior and learning problems, and increase the possibility of miscarriages and infertility. Nussle gave interviews to the press and presented her findings at the North American Congress of Clinical Toxicology the following year. The shocking data got US health professionals and the media talking about La Oroya's children.

Soon after Nussle and other Ohio Presbyterians had gathered their preliminary data, Ellie Stock, pastor of a Joining Hands member congregation in St. Louis, traveled to Peru to see La Oroya for herself. "It looked surreal, like a moonscape," she said. "The vegetation had died, and the orange-colored Mantaro River was dead—all due to the contamination. Grey flakes drifted down from the sky, covered our clothing, and burned our eyes and throats."

Stock and her colleagues gave seminars for La Oroya pastors on Scripture's mandate to care for God's creation. She received friends from La Oroya into her St. Louis home, and she organized a prayer vigil for La Oroya's children.

On a wintry Saturday morning in February 2003, Stock introduced Hinostroza to Fernando Serrano, a researcher at St. Louis University's School of Public Health. Stock also introduced Hinostroza to a group of health advocates from Herculaneum, Missouri, a nearby town struggling with pollution from another Doe Run Company metal smelter. Within a year two health advocates from Herculaneum—a Catholic and a Presbyterian—would travel to Lima to testify before Peru's Congress. St. Louis University (SLU) and the Centers for Disease Control also agreed to organize a major environmental health study for La Oroya to provide scientific data on the city's pollution.

Then Hinostroza pleaded for help from Monsignor Pedro Barreto, the Catholic archbishop of Huancayo, Peru. "Monsignor, we know that we adults are already contaminated and many of us are sick," Hinostroza said. "But we are here for the children. And you must help us because this is what Jesus would do."

Moved to tears, the Jesuit archbishop offered his assistance.

Barreto studied the issue, spoke with all sides of the growing conflict, and invited SLU to conduct an independent study as the first step in an open process to reduce pollution in La Oroya and the entire Mantaro River Valley. The results, presented in December 2005, showed that Hinostroza and La Oroya's parents had good reason to worry about the town's pollution. More than 97 percent of the city's twelve thousand children had lead poisoning. In addition, high amounts of arsenic, cadmium, and other toxins significantly increased residents' risk of cancer.

Doe Run says it is working to "find solutions" to the city's environmental and health problems, which were left by "previous operators of the La Oroya complex." The company, which has operated the smelter since 1997, says it "is concerned with the impact the contamination has on the surrounding communities as well as the health concerns brought on by poor nutrition, lack of sanitation and clean water, and poor air quality."

The SLU study began to change the Peruvian government's indifference to the situation. CBS News, *Vanity Fair*, *The New York Times*, and more than five hundred US and Peruvian newspapers and magazines reported on the story, putting pressure on the Peruvian government.

Peru's Supreme Court ruled in the summer of 2006 that the government's health ministry was negligent in protecting La Oroya's children and ordered it to implement an emergency health plan. Cleanup has been slow, and Doe Run has asked for more time to implement the government's mandated pollution controls. Still, the improvements brought about by these groups have been measurable.

Peruvian and North American Christians together played a key role in reducing La Oroya's pollution, beginning cleaning, and alerting authorities and residents of the pollution's dangers. What started as one woman's cry for help mushroomed into a global mission effort across denominational lines and national borders. The mission effort went beyond financial and spiritual support as Christians offered, not only their faith, but also access to scientific information and the media.

Two-way Ministry

The work in La Oroya also led to a serendipity: because of Peru's mission history, Peruvian Catholics and Protestants have often considered each other to be nonbelievers. One of the tangible results of the mission in La Oroya has been a surprising unity among Peruvian and US believers, including evangelical lay pastors and a Jesuit archbishop, North American missionaries and Pentecostal mothers, Dominican nuns and Presbyterian congregations.

Dietrich Bonhoeffer asked, "Will the church merely gather up those whom the wheel has crushed, or will it prevent the wheel from crushing them?" Hinostroza and Javier—together with hundreds of Christians in Peru and the United States—are learning the answer to that timely question.

_____

Hunter Farrell lived in Peru as a missionary with his wife and three children for nine years and worked with the Joining Hands Network of Peru. He is now director of Presbyterian World Mission. "Cleaning Up La Oroya" was first published by Christianity Today *on April 20, 2007.*

■ Open Up

Select one of these activities to launch your discussion time.

Option 1

Discuss these icebreaker questions:

- Share three ways you use environmental resources to improve or benefit your life. For example, you would not survive without water.

- What would you do if the environmental resources you depend on were not available or were suddenly harmful to you? How would you feel in this situation?

Option 2

We all benefit from the environment in many ways. Form pairs and take some time to look through magazines with photos of natural scenes. With your partner, use black markers to write directly on the pictures different ways we benefit from the environmental resources portrayed in the images. For example, you might circle the leaves of a tree and write, "Provides oxygen."

After several minutes, gather back together as a larger group and share what you wrote in your pairs. Then discuss:

- How would it affect your life if one or more of these environmental benefits were no longer available to you?

■ The Issue

In Hunter Farrell's "Cleaning Up La Oroya" we learn that some especially vulnerable people are affected by the environmental impacts perpetuated largely by others.

- How might environmental issues be linked to our mandate to love God and our neighbor?

■ Reflect

Take a moment to read the following Scriptures: Psalm 104:10–31; Isaiah 1:15–17; and Matthew 22:34–40. Jot down a few observations about the passages: Do you see a link between them? Are there similar themes or ideas? What do these passages say about harm to the environment?

■ Let's Explore

When we degrade the environment, God's purpose for creation is affected.

Imagine life in a village with a clean and healthy river running through it. Keep this image in your mind while someone reads aloud Psalm 104:10–17.

In Farrell's article about La Oroya, a St. Louis-based pastor describes the Peruvian village. Allow the image you had in your mind to be transformed as you consider this description from the article:

It was surreal, like a moonscape . . . The vegetation had died, and the orange-colored Mantaro River was dead—all due to the contamination [from the nearby smelter plant]. Grey flakes drifted down from the sky, covered our clothing, and burned our eyes and throats.

- What's your gut reaction when you see natural resources damaged by industrialization, urban sprawl, or pollution? Share an example of a place you've seen or visited that's been "ruined" by humans.

- Review Psalm 104:10–31. How does this psalm characterize God's purposes for creation? How were those purposes affected by the operations of the smelter plant in La Oroya?

- Farrell's article discusses numerous physical effects to this environmental transformation—headaches, fatigue, cancer, and more. What might be some of the spiritual effects? Explain.

The National Council of Churches USA has said,

We have tilled ungraciously and kept God's covenant badly. We have not honored the covenant between God and every living creature. Through polluting air, land, and water, through stripping the earth of non-renewable resources, through relentless consumption of natural resources, and through exploiting God's people, we do damage to the creation that God created and called good. (*Environmental Racism: A Study Guide*)

- What's your response to the idea that environmental degradation disrupts God's purposes for creation? Explain your point of view.

Caring for creation is part of loving God and our neighbors.

In La Oroya, the environment not only ceased to sustain life, but—due to contamination from the smelter plant—began to harm life. When the Joining Hands Network learned of this, they knew that the issues and problems were beyond their abilities to solve them. Still, they responded by visiting the community.

Read Matthew 22:34–40.

- Why do you think the Joining Hands Network reached out to their faraway "neighbors"? What moved them beyond compassionate thoughts to Christian action?

- Describe a situation in which you reached out to someone in need even though you were not sure what to do.

- How do you think you would have responded to a plea for assistance with environmental pollution? Why?

One pastor responded poignantly to a meeting with a seven-year-old boy named Javier, who suffered from relentless headaches and fatigue, saying, "Our children would be like Javier if we lived here."

- When have you seen your neighbor's problem as your own, like the pastor in this example?

- Take a moment to consider environmental problems you know about, perhaps from your own community. Who do these problems affect? What, if any, connection do you see between yourself and those people? How do God's "greatest commandments" affect the way you see those environmental problems?

God's concern for justice is also an environmental concern.

In R. Scott Nolen's article on climate change, published in *Christianity Today*, he says, "Although industrialized nations are primarily responsible for the emissions, developing countries and the poor are most vulnerable to global warming's destructive effects."

Bill McKibben, in a sermon titled, "The Comforting Whirlwind: God and the Environmental Crisis," puts it less mildly. He says,

> We in this country create 25 percent of the world's carbon dioxide. It is the affluent lifestyles that we lead that overwhelmingly contribute to this problem. And to call it a problem is to understate what it really is: it is a crime. A crime against the poorest and most marginalized people on this planet. We've never figured out, though God knows we've tried, a more effective way to destroy their lives. (*Cry of Creation*)

Read Isaiah 1:15–17. In this passage, God berates his people for performing acts of worship while living lives of great injustice toward the needy and oppressed.

- In light of this scripture, what is your response to Bill McKibben's comments? Do you agree with him? Why or why not?

- In light of this scripture, what is your response to Farrell's article about the toxic contamination in La Oroya by a US-based international corporation? Do you feel God calling you to respond to problems and injustices like the pollution in La Oroya? If so, how?

Farrell's article concludes with these words from Dietrich Bonhoeffer: "Will the church merely gather up those whom the wheel has crushed, or will it prevent the wheel from crushing them?"

- How can the church play a role in preventing the wheel of environmental destruction from crushing people?

■ Going Forward

Form pairs to discuss these questions:

- What are some of the most important roles that God's creation plays in your life?

- What can you do to show God how important his creation is to your life? To the lives of your neighbors?

With your partner, read the "Do Your Part" box below. Brainstorm several other actions a person can take to care for creation. Then commit to doing at least one action, and tell your partner about your commitment. For example, you may commit to riding your bike to work at least once per week.

Pray together for those who are directly affected by environmental degradation and for the motivation to follow through on your commitments.

DO YOUR PART

Here are several things you can do this week to care for creation:

- Pray that communities affected by environmental degradation will receive assistance, justice, and renewal.

- Reduce the chemical load on the planet by using homemade cleansers at home. For example, mix vinegar and water to make your own window cleanser. Flush your drain by pouring in baking soda followed by vinegar or lemon juice. See http://www.earth-easy.com/live_nontoxic_solutions.htm#substitutions for more. Also switch to organic, non-toxic lawn and gardening treatments. See http://www.dirtdoctor.com/ for tips.

- Walk, bike, carpool, or use public transportation whenever possible, and combine errands to make one trip in the car rather than making multiple trips.

- "Tithe" your carbon dioxide—give up 10 percent of your carbon dioxide usage through recycling, minimizing air conditioning, using less hot water, using a clothesline instead of a dryer, switching to fluorescent lights, and eating locally grown food.

- Use electricity produced by green power if it is available in your area.

- Conduct a home energy audit. See http://www.eere.energy.gov/consumer/your_home/energy_audits/index.cfm/mytopic=11170 for details.

How can the food we eat

help or hurt God's creation?

| SCRIPTURE FOCUS | Romans 14:1–4,13–23 |
| | 1 Corinthians 8:1–13 |

KITCHEN-SINK

ENVIRONMENTALISM

■

You plan a wonderful meal and invite a number
of acquaintances to share it with you. And then you
notice: Sam hasn't taken any pork. "Is he vegetarian?"
you wonder. Ruthy asks where you acquired asparagus
in November. "I got it at the supermarket," you mention.
Ruthy's eyes widen, "No, I mean, where was it grown?
We don't have the climate to grow asparagus in North
America during late fall. A lot of carbon emissions were
produced transporting this asparagus to the upper
Midwest." Walter mentions the corn shortage as he bites
into his cornbread, "More and more corn is being grown
to produce ethanol," he mutters. "People in Mexico
are starting to go hungry. They can't afford tortillas."
And when you bring out the strawberry shortcake,
everyone requests it with no strawberries.

Prudence nods at the strawberries with one
word, "Pesticides."

Perhaps people's responses are a bit exaggerated here, but there's truth in this story. More and more North Americans are starting to realize the environmental implications of what we put into our mouths. And it's a daunting realization that can cause immediate, dramatic action, apathy, or an overwhelming feeling of guilt and responsibility.

In today's study we'll read "Dining Dilemmas" by Cindy Crosby and explore new ways of eating with God's creation foremost in our thoughts.

■ Before You Meet

Read "Dining Dilemmas" by Cindy Crosby.

DINING DILEMMAS

How shall we then eat?

A review of Michael Pollan's *The Omnivore's Dilemma: A Natural History of Four Meals*

by Cindy Crosby

True confessions: I love McDonald's French fries. They're a guilty pleasure. I also enjoy shopping at Whole Foods, the organic grocery chain in my neighborhood. I feel virtuous loading my cart with brown eggs laid by happy chickens in comfortable nests, or eating beef from free-range cows. When I pull a can of Amy's Organic Soup from the shelves I envision Amy and her grandma in an eighteenth-century restored farmhouse kitchen chopping tomatoes and adjusting spices.

Whole Foods makes a large dent in my pocketbook that I rationalize by saying I'm supporting family farms and putting my money where my mouth is about agricultural reform and organics. Very righteous of me,

I'm sure. But true culinary sainthood arrives when I make a pot of chili with the heirloom tomatoes frozen from my garden last summer, or pull a few green spring onions for a dinner salad. I've even been known to fry up some "dandelion fritters" from our yard, in which the yellow flowers are a star attraction. (We're on shaky terms with some of our suburban neighbors.) This, I think, is eating at its best—fresh, local, and organic.

When I began reading *The Omnivore's Dilemma: A Natural History of Four Meals* by Michael Pollan, I realized I had some rethinking to do. In this doorstopper of a book, Pollan, a longtime contributing writer to *The New York Times Magazine* and now a professor of journalism at University of California in Berkley, traces the path of four meals through their various systems: organic food, alternative food, industrial food (such as fast food), and food we forage for ourselves. In *The Omnivore's Dilemma*, Pollan tackles some daunting questions. What ethics are involved in our food choices? What impact do they have on the environment? And who or what are we subsidizing with our food choices?

In his first section, devoted to convenience food, Pollan traces much of the cheap food America eats (and the plight of American agriculture) to the super-abundance and government subsidizing of corn. His research is startling. Corn has found its way into a large percentage of the foods we eat: canned fruit, mayonnaise, vitamins, and cake mixes just for starters, raising a myriad of questions. How could a McDonald's chicken nugget be composed of thirty-eight ingredients, thirteen derived from corn? What does it mean to eat beef, chicken, or even salmon largely raised on corn?

Pollan shows that corn-fed animals and fish don't have the same nutritional value as grass-fed animals; farmed salmon, for example, do not have the same omega-3 levels as their wild counterparts. By changing the diet of the animals we raise, we are changing ourselves. And it only takes a look at the soaring obesity rates to realize it is not for the better.

But the two portions of *The Omnivore's Dilemma* that I found most engaging explored the organic food industry (an oxymoron in itself) and sustainable farming. In the segment on sustainable agriculture (which he comes closest to idealizing of any of the four food systems), Pollan lauds a small Christian operation called Polyface Farms in Virginia as a model of what agriculture can aspire to. By using a more holistic, humane approach to land use and consuming locally and seasonally, rather than globally, sustainable farming seems to solve many of the problems created by industrial agriculture. Good reading, although many will wonder if it's viable on a large scale. To function on an ongoing basis, this sort of agriculture requires a heart-and-mind change on the part of the *consumer*. No small thing.

When Pollan examines the organic grocery business—"Big Organic"—he had me from the first page. What does organic *really* mean? With Wal-mart's recent announcement that it's jumping into the organic foods world, we need to know. And if I'm justifying my budget-busting trips to Whole Foods in the name of God, small-farming, and sustainable agriculture, I don't want to be hoodwinked.

Pollan traces the organic foods movement back to the writings of Sir Albert Howard, whose 1940 *An Agricultural Testament* informed Rodale's magazine *Organic Gardening and Farming* and the writings of Wendell Berry (who is quoted liberally through Pollan's book). Howard had the arresting idea that we need to treat "the whole problem of health in soil, plant, animal and man as one great subject." With this in mind, Pollan takes a deeper look at where the food from places such as Whole Foods *now* comes from. He also looks at such oddities as "organic microwavable TV dinners" and the article by nutritionist Joan Dye Gussow, "Can an Organic Twinkie Be Certified?" (The answer is yes.) This is journalism at its best.

Then Pollan, a master wordsmith, takes on the genre he calls Supermarket Pastoral, "a most seductive literary form, beguiling enough to survive in the face of a great many discomfiting facts." Why so? "I suspect . . . it gratifies some of our deepest, oldest longings, not merely for safe food, but for a connection to the earth and to the handful of domesticated creatures we've long depended on. Whole Foods understands all this better than we do." What about dairy farms where cows have "access to pasture?" What exactly is "pasture?" And what is "access?" What is a "free-range chicken?" (The term, Pollan shows through a fascinating trip through a poultry house, is largely a joke, an empty conceit.)

Petroleum is another problem. What about the ethics of trucking "organically grown asparagus from Argentina" to America's suburbs in January? What are the economics of fuel and the cost to the people of Argentina, whose land is feeding Americans? The food industry, Pollan points out, burns nearly a fifth of all the petroleum consumed in the United States. And most "organic farming" is done on organic industrial farms, a contradiction in terms that Pollan explores at length in the fields of California. "Is there anything wrong with this picture? I'm not sure, frankly," Pollan concludes. What he finds is "a much greener machine, but a machine, nonetheless."

I won't feel nearly so virtuous the next time I shop at Whole Foods.

Foraging is the subject of the last section of the book, which owes most of its charm to Pollan's willingness to learn to hunt wild game, something he's fairly squeamish about. Some of his writing as he forages for mushrooms is particularly lyrical.

So what do we do with this information? How shall we then eat? If I'm honest, I'll confess that I probably won't give up my occasional bag of McDonald's French fries, and I'll still cruise the aisles at Whole Foods, albeit less sentimentally. How do I redeem this?

Perhaps, as Pollan writes, the best way to fight industrial eating is to recall people to the superior pleasure of traditional foods enjoyed communally. Then, our eating contributes to the survival of landscapes and species and traditional foods that would otherwise succumb to the "one world, one taste" fast food ideal. Having a diversified food economy where consumers have access to thriving alternative food sources, he concludes, allows us to withstand shocks to the system: outbreaks of mad cow disease, petroleum running out, pesticides that quit working.

It's possible to live with contradictions in how we eat, Pollan believes, but it's important that we face up to our compromises. For me, this means planting a little more garden to offset my occasional golden arches French fry consumption; thinking more seriously about taking out that local farm share at the cooperative down the road; and inviting friends over for "slow" dinners and conversation more often. In a fallen world, we take baby steps on the journey back to wholeness.

_____

Cindy Crosby is the author of three books, including By Willoway Brook: Exploring the Landscape of Prayer *(Paraclete), and is editor/compiler of* Ancient Christian Devotional—A Year of Weekly Readings *(InterVarsity Press). "Dining Dilemmas" was originally published in full online by* Christianity Today *in June, 2006.)*

■ Open Up

Select one of these activities to launch your discussion time.

Option 1

Discuss these icebreaker questions:

- What is your favorite food in the world?

- Share one of your best food memories. What made it so memorable? The food? The people? The atmosphere?

- What considerations influence why you eat what you do? In other words, what are your "food priorities"? Price? Convenience? Taste? Preference?

- Have you ever been challenged to consider the environmental implications of your food choices? What happened? Did anything in your life change? Why or why not?

Option 2

Before you meet, plan to have a group potluck before your discussion. Assign different people to bring the food: main entrée, bread or potatoes, vegetables, salad, and dessert. As you eat together, share stories of interesting potlucks you've participated in and times of celebration over meals with others.

■ The Issue

Food is a topic everyone has an opinion about. Many people love to talk about food: recipes they've tried, food they like, food they dislike, diets they're on. Everyone likes to talk about food because everyone eats. Eating is one of the primary shared activities of humankind—even more than sex—because every person must do it in order to stay alive.

In today's article, we read a book review that discusses how we think about eating.

- What were some ideas mentioned in this article that you had never considered before? How did you respond to them?

- Cindy Crosby writes about both her fondness for McDonald's French fries and her romanticized visits to Whole Foods Market. She notes that this is a contradiction of experience. Where are the contradictions about food in your own life?

Surprisingly, the Bible has a lot to say about what people eat. From the creation of the first garden in Genesis 1 to Levitical food laws to food controversy in the early church, our Scriptures encompass many cultural and historical ideas about what it means to be people who eat. Let's look at some of these texts in-depth and see what they may say to us today.

■ Reflect

Take a moment to read Romans 14:1–4, 13–23 and 1 Corinthians 8:1–13 on your own. Also read the "In Context" box below. Jot down a few notes about these passages. How might they speak to food issues today? What questions do they raise for you?

IN CONTEXT: 1 CORINTHIANS 8

First Corinthians is an epistle, written by Paul to the church in Corinth. The city was located on the nine kilometer bit of land located between the Gulf of Corinth (Ionian Sea) and the Saronic Gulf (Agean Sea), so it was perfectly situated for industry and trade, which made it a wealthy Roman colony. The ancient Corinthian culture shares many attributes with contemporary culture, including competitiveness, achievement, self-promotion, and a tendency to value knowledge and freedom over love and respect for others. In short, Corinth was a modern, diverse, cosmopolitan city with many successful entrepreneurs and a spirit of consumerism.

Paul had stayed in Corinth for about eighteen months in A.D. 50–51, and when he left, he continued to receive news from the church via Apollos, letters of inquiry sent by the church, and "Chloe's people" (1 Corinthians 1:11). First Corinthians is a response to much of this communication, and chapter 8 is directly related to "the matters about which you wrote" (7:1).

Note adapted from "Food Sacrificed to Idols" by Joy-Elizabeth Lawrence in Eat Well: A Food Road Map *(published by *culture is not optional). © Joy-Elizabeth Lawrence, used with permission.*

■ Let's Explore

We must find our identity in Christ rather than the types of food we eat.

Read 1 Corinthians 8:1–13.

At first glance, 1 Corinthians 8 may not seem applicable to our lives today; after all, we aren't faced with the choice of whether or not to eat meat that's been sacrificed to false gods. But the underlying theme of Paul's message to the Corinthians about food *can* speak to us today as we navigate our culture's messages about food and its importance in our lives.

- What does the fact that Paul addresses the church's question say about the importance of what we eat? Do you think this issue is as important as some of the other topics addressed in this epistle, like marriage, worship, sexual behavior, and church unity? Explain.

- What's most significant in these texts: food or people's treatment of each other? Or both? Why?

It's important to understand that most meat available during this time was meat that had first been butchered at a temple. The temple was sort of the one-stop-shop for all your meat and worship needs. So, to not eat meat sacrificed to idols meant more than avoiding one store. It meant avoiding almost all meat.

Review Romans 14:1–4, 13–23.

- How would you summarize the arguments about the strong and the weak in Romans 14 and 1 Corinthians 8? What is each group saying? How does each group have a point?

Just like "the strong" and "the weak" were identifying themselves by what they ate (or did not eat), people today choose personal food identities, such as "vegetarian," "raw foodist" or even "I don't eat that healthy stuff!" that gives them a specific food-identity.

- In your opinion, is having a "food-identity" problematic? Imagine ways food-identities could be divisive in the church today or share personal experiences in which food-identities have caused discomfort or division in relationships.

Some biblical commentators note that the word often translated as "conscience" in 1 Corinthians 8:10–11 would better be understood as "self-awareness." If we read it in this way, the issue of food sacrificed to idols becomes more about one's identity than a moral choice, so that eating or not eating meat sacrificed to idols directly affects one's identity as a Christ-follower.

- If we read these texts with the connotation of self-identity rather than "moral choice" in mind, how does it change the meaning? What do you think about this perspective?

Food has the power to unite or separate.

- Have you ever had a local food experience (such as visiting a farmer's market, shopping at a roadside farm stand, or eating produce from your own garden)? If so, describe what it was like.

- What sorts of things do you consider when making food choices? What motivates you to eat what you do?

In his article "Eating Locally," written for *Christianity Today*, Ragan Sutterfield starts off by saying:

Last year, *Gourmet* magazine editor and veteran food-writer Ruth Reichel asked the question—local or organic? "Eating organically is a wonderful thing," [Reichel] wrote, "but once you start calculating the real cost of food, you begin to think about the expense of flying it halfway around the world. What price do we pay in fuel, in government subsidies, in loss of flavor? Perhaps most importantly, what does it cost our community when we support people in other places at the expense of our neighbors?"

These are questions widely asked today in the sustainable food movement, whose slogan has become: "local is the new organic."

• What examples can you think of that answer Reichel's question, "What does it cost our community when we support people in other places at the expense of our neighbors?" How does this unite or separate communities?

In Romans 14:20, we read, "All foods are all right to eat, but it is wrong to eat food that causes someone else to sin."

• Does this mean that there are no moral implications for our food choices today? What about factory farming? What about misuse of soil? Inhumanely treated livestock? Deceptive food marketing? Share your opinion on whether or not the food we eat—and how it is created—is a moral issue.

• What are the sorts of ways what we eat could cause someone else to stumble? What are contemporary ways that food divides or unites people?

We must consider our responsibility as stewards.

Cindy Crosby notes that,

> Perhaps, as Pollan writes, the best way to fight industrial eating is to recall people to the superior pleasure of traditional foods enjoyed communally. Then, our eating contributes to the survival of landscapes and species and traditional foods that would otherwise succumb to the 'one world, one taste' fast food ideal. Having a diversified food economy where consumers have access to thriving alternative food sources, he concludes, allows us to withstand shocks to the system: outbreaks of mad cow disease, petroleum running out, pesticides that quit working.

• Brainstorm together some ways you could help steward our food system, the land, or what and how you eat. What sorts of stewardship choices are you already making about food? (Remember: price is not the bottom line in stewardship! Often, injustice masquerades as thrift.)

• Of course there are many things we can do to help the environment with our food choices, but what other benefits would these choices bring?

■ Going Forward

Examining all the problems with the contemporary food system in North America can be a depressing experience. But don't feel guilty if you hadn't considered these issues until now! Use this as an opportunity to change your life, and the lives around you, for the better. You don't have to change everything at once, of course, but begin experimenting incrementally. Do so in an attitude of worship, not coercion.

• In today's reading or discussion, did you think of any change you could make about how and what you eat? What is it? Will you act on it? When?

• Next time you participate in an observance of communion, think about the issue of food today. How do you think this might affect your experience of communion?

Gather in pairs and read the "Do Your Part" box below. Discuss together any changes you want to make in your life, then pray with your partner. Thank God for the food he provides for us. Pray we'll all be good stewards.

DO YOUR PART

Still overwhelmed? Choose one of the following ideas to try. Then, later, add another idea.

- Avoid wasting food. Americans waste tons of food everyday. When you go home, clean out your cupboard and refrigerator. What food is still okay but needs to be eaten soon? Use up that food this week or donate the dry goods to a food bank. If you are more mindful about eating leftovers, you'll use fewer food resources and save money.

- Shop at a local farmer's market. Find out when a local farmer's market occurs in your city. Go to the market and bring cash and your own bags or basket. Buy vegetables. Talk to the farmers; find out where they live, what they grow, and how they grow it.

- Learn to "put up." Like a particular food a lot, like strawberries or asparagus? When it's in season, freeze, can, or even pickle produce you like. Then, you can eat it year-round without it having to be transported halfway across the world.

- Eat a weed. There are quite a few edible weeds that grow in North America, including dandelions, purslane, wild chives, and lambs quarters. Google "edible weeds" to find pictures of them and even recipes to help you prepare them.

- Avoid packaged foods. Packaged foods use more resources to prepare and transport, and they have fewer health benefits than homemade foods. Try making something you usually purchase (hummus, pizza crust, bread, or pudding).

Is animal rights

a religious issue?

SCRIPTURE FOCUS

Genesis 1:20–28; 2:18–20

Isaiah 11:6–9

Matthew 6:26

A BIBLICAL

VIEW OF ANIMALS

■

When a mosquito lands on your arm, do you want to smash it? Or do you respect its life as a creature of God?

Do you feel discomfort—or even a strong sense of disgust or injustice—when you learn about livestock living awful lives in atrocious conditions on factory farms?

When you take a prescription medicine which was developed using animal testing (including animal death), are you bothered? Or does animal suffering in the name of science seem justified to you?

Some of these questions may seem silly, but many Christian animal-rights activists are demanding that we address this issue: is every living creature so sacred that as humans we have no right to harm them—much less kill them? In this study, you'll explore what the Bible says (and *doesn't* say) about animal rights during your discussion of Tim Stafford's *Christianity Today* article "Animal Lib."

■ Before You Meet

Read "Animal Lib" by Tim Stafford from *Christianity Today*.

ANIMAL LIB

Despite silliness and fanaticism on both sides, the animal-rights debate remains an inherently religious issue.

by Tim Stafford

The animal-rights movement raises questions about more than animals. Ultimately, it raises the question of whether a secular society can make sense of itself.

An image: I am eleven years old, and on a bright, spring day I stand on the banks of an irrigation ditch that runs near my school. Someone has caught a frog, and two boys are taking turns throwing their pocketknives at it. I can catch only occasional glimpses of the frog through the legs of my peers, who are crowding around, eager to see.

After many tries, a knife finds its target, and the crowd lets out an admiring groan. I press closer. The frog, split open, is leaking its guts. Still living, it scrabbles weakly in the dust. I turn away feeling sick and guilty. I know without a shadow of a doubt that what I have seen is wrong. This should never be done to a frog.

Another image: I am thirty-one years old, and on another bright, spring day I watch a goat die. I am in Kenya, and as is traditional in East African celebrations, a goat is being slaughtered for a barbecue. I have eaten meat right out of the cellophane all my life, but I have never seen a mammal die. So I stand with a huddle of African friends, watching the deed with horrified fascination. It is done quickly, without cruelty. The neck is slit and blood spurts out. The goat bleats, struggles, and then lies still. It is gutted, skinned, cut apart. Nothing is wasted. The intestines are cooked; the head goes into a pot for soup. The meat, even after it is cut into pieces for the grill, has a habit of twitching.

I feel a little shaken by what I have seen. I do not feel ashamed, but I do feel solemn. It is not a light thing to take an animal's life.

Confronting "Speciesism"

Almost everyone would accept what my eleven-year-old mind concluded about the needless death of a frog: it was wrong.

About the death of the goat, not all would agree. Most people have thought that as long as the goat was killed for food, and did not suffer more than necessary, its killing was justified. A persistent minority, however, has questioned our right to use animals for our own ends, as though they were merely "things."

Despite such differences of opinion, virtually all Western people have worked from the Christian premise that human beings were set apart by God for a special purpose and for special responsibilities. We are worth more than the animals, and we must act better than animals—so we have believed. Those who wanted to protect animals from suffering worked from this assumption, as did those who justified using and eating animals.

But no more. Today, the most visible animal-rights activists speak out against the belief that humankind has been put in charge of creation. This presumption, they claim, has led to the overwhelming slavery and abuse of animals. They scoff at the Christian requirement that we treat animals kindly. It is, they say, like the requirement that slave owners treat their slaves kindly. The activists' goal is to set the animals free— free from all human control and domination.

"Humane treatment is simply sentimental, sympathetic patronage," says Michael W. Fox, a veterinarian who directs the Center for the Respect of Life and Environment at the Humane Society of the United States.

Tom Regan, a well-known activist, puts it this way: "The animal-rights philosophy is abolitionist rather than reformist. It's not better cages we work for, but empty cages." Gary Francione, a law professor who litigates animal-rights cases, would not allow an animal to suffer even if the research led to a cancer cure: "I don't believe it is morally permissible to exploit weaker beings even if we derive benefits."

In a *Harper's* magazine forum on the morality of animal experimentation, the theoretical possibility of implanting a pig's heart to save a human baby's life was raised. One animal-rights activist, who is sternly against such a possibility, said that the baby's parents should be made to care about the pig. When another participant exclaimed, "I don't want to change [the parents'] reaction. I want human beings to care about babies," Ingrid Newkirk, head of People for the Ethical Treatment of Animals, retorted, "Like racism or sexism, that remark is pure speciesism."

Speciesism, a term invented in Peter Singer's foundational text, *Animal Liberation,* is the allegedly bigoted contention that human beings are more important than other animals. "It can no longer be maintained by anyone but a religious fanatic that man is the special darling of the universe," Singer wrote, "or that other animals were created to provide us with food, or that we have divine authority over them and divine permission to kill them."

That makes animal rights one of the first social movements to claim an explicitly non-Christian point of view. Not all its members share this ideology, but the most publicized leaders speak against long-held Christian assumptions. Michael Fox, quoted in *The Washingtonian,* put it succinctly: "There are no clear distinctions between us and animals. Animals communicate, animals have emotions, animals can think. Some thinkers believe that the human soul is different because we are immortal, and that just becomes completely absurd." Humane Society literature, according to writer Katie McCabe, has claimed since 1980 that "there is no rational basis for maintaining a moral distinction between the treatment of humans and other animals."

Sputtering and Fuming

It is tempting to focus on the abrupt twists and turns in the logic of animal-rights activists. They point to science's inability to document absolute differences between human and beast. But this hardly suggests that we should treat animals well. It should be instructive to note that animals eat each other: that is, whales eat seals, seals eat fish, all without evident taint of "speciesism." Clearly, to animal-rights activists, human beings are special—special in their responsibility to treat animals better than many animals treat each other. The animal-rights movement would like to raise animals to the moral status of humans. It would be just as *logical* to lower humans to the moral status of animals.

But why hold animal-rights activists to a higher standard of logic than their opponents? The philosophy of animal rights does not seem coherent, but as a number of thinkers have noted, a secular philosophy of human rights has yet to prove coherent either.

This is quite noticeable in the back-and-forth between animal-rights activists and the scientists, government officials, and journalists who confront them. Both sides argue fervently from a position firmly planted in the air. The activists ask: What gives humankind the right to decide an animal's fate? Why should a monkey lose its life to save a child? In response, the sages of our society sputter and fume.

Scientists have been amazed and outraged as the protests of what they regard as a lunatic fringe have disturbed the sanctity of their laboratories. Although typically not philosophically inclined, scientists do have a solemn sense of purpose in what they do. This gets expressed in various ways. At the high end is the philosophical: we are pursuing the truth, they say. At the low end is the pragmatic: we are saving lives through medicine.

It is at the low end that scientists usually try to meet the animal-rights activists. John Kaplan, writing in *Science,* suggests that scientists show photos of "human burn victims or of quadriplegics to offset the pathetic pictures of the animals used in the research." He assumes that people will favor the suffering of animals over the suffering of human beings, and he is probably right about that.

But as far as the activists are concerned, this begs the question. What right have we to make an animal suffer in our place? We would not consider it right to treat another human being that way. Why an animal? What makes us think we are so special?

Ironically, the biologists proclaiming urgently that every delay in their experiments may cost human lives are members of the discipline that has been at pains to show there is no dramatic difference between humans and other animals, that different species are merely different products of evolution. By their own criteria, one is not "better" than another.

But now scientists have made a different discovery: in their heart of hearts they believe that human beings are morally different from animals. Only they cannot say why they think so. They can only sputter with outrage that anyone would put a human being on the same level as a pig.

Dangerous Thinking

A *Newsweek* cover story ended with these remarks on vivisection:

> The question is whether the practical benefits of vivisection consti-
> tute a moral justification for it. If mankind's interest in finding a better
> treatment for AIDS doesn't justify conducting lethal experiments on
> individual humans, an ethicist might ask, why does it justify performing
> them on monkeys? Why doesn't a monkey deserve moral consider-
> ation? What is the relevant difference between a human subject and
> an animal subject?
>
> To reply that the human is human and the animal isn't only begs
> the question . . .
>
> Another possible answer is that we humans enjoy certain God-
> given prerogatives. We are, after all, the only creatures the Bible says
> were made in God's image . . .
>
> It may be a difference, but it's not an empirical, observable one. It
> has to be taken on faith . . .
>
> Maybe *there is no reasoned moral justification* [italics added] . . .
> Whatever the answer, scientists can no longer afford to pretend that
> their critics' moral concerns are frivolous. Profound questions are being
> raised, and ignoring them won't make them go away.

On that uncertain note, the long article ended. On a similar note, a *New Republic* article by Robert Wright essentially accepted the argument that no moral distinction can be made between animals and humans. The belief that humans are in a special category, wrote Wright, "is a perfectly fine thing to believe, but it's hard to argue for. It depends much more on religious conviction than on any plausible line of reasoning." And of course, Wright assumed, religious conviction was ruled out of reasonable discussion.

Unfortunately, Wright also showed where his assumptions can lead: "Human rights . . . isn't some divine law imparted to us from above or some Platonic truth apprehended through the gift of reason. The idea of individual rights is simply a non-aggression pact . . . It's a deal struck for mutual convenience."

Wright showed the danger of excluding religion from questions that are inherently religious. Investigating animal rights through pure logic, without revelation, can easily turn against human rights, and ultimately against animals. If human rights are merely "a deal struck for mutual convenience," then anybody who doesn't buy into the deal (Stalin, say) is morally free to go his or her own way. And of course it makes no sense at all to extend the deal to animals, whose protection and care is certainly not a matter of mutual convenience. Humans will only care for animals if they believe that it is a calling, not a "deal."

As Richard John Neuhaus has put it, "The campaign against 'speciesism' is a campaign against the singularity of human dignity and, therefore, of human responsibility . . . The hope for a more humane world, including the more humane treatment of animals, is premised upon what they deny."

Opponents of animal-rights activists also sometimes fall into logic that is inherently dangerous. Why should medical researchers sacrifice animals for human welfare? Journalist Katie McCabe suggests an answer of sorts in her *Washingtonian* exposé of animal rights activists, "Beyond Cruelty." She points out that the debate "has been framed . . . as everything but what it really is—a moral argument that penetrates to the definition of humanity." She then quotes businessman Richard Kelly: The debate "is not an argument that philosophy or religion or even science can solve . . . In the end, human beings and their needs are the only argument that matters."

This is a kind of "defending my family" argument. It goes, "I don't know who's better, them or us. But I know that if I have to choose, I'm fighting for us." This *is* pure speciesism, if you please. *Anything that enhances, protects, or increases the joy of the human race is good. Why? Because it's my team.* This is a form of humanism that justifies animal experiments, but a great deal more—too much more. There is no limit to what it will justify in the name of the human race.

What we see through the lens of this controversy is a society that has lost faith in the religious view it was built on and has nothing suitable to put in its place. The religious sentiments continue—on the part of animal-rights activists (the sympathy for animal suffering) and on the part of scientists (the belief in human preeminence)—but the sentiments have lost their foundation. When someone challenges them, the response is the agitated indignation of people who are sure they are doing the right thing, though they cannot say why. Animal-rights activists cannot articulate why they care about the death of a frog or the death of a child. Nor can scientists say why they would kill a frog to save a child. They argue from feeling—a feeling that banks on thousands of years of a faith in which they no longer believe.

The Spectrum of Christian Thought

Despite all efforts to rule religion out, the debate over animal rights remains inherently and fundamentally religious. That is not to say, however, that religion offers only one answer. Hinduism, for example, has its own view, to which some animal-rights activists are attracted. And within Christianity there is room for tremendous differences—room for the chicken farmer viewing his birds as meat-making machines, as well as for Saint Francis preaching sermons to them.

The chicken farmer claims familiar scriptural supports. According to his view, God intended animals to serve human ends, and it is no cruelty to use them for their created purpose. Genesis 1 describes how humankind was charged with ruling "over the fish of the sea and the birds of the air . . . and over all the creatures that move along the ground" (v. 26, NIV). Genesis 9:3, furthermore, records how God gave all living creatures to Noah and his family for food. Biblical people—including Jesus—were flesh eaters. They were also animal users—shepherds and fishermen and dirt farmers who used animals to plow and thresh. The Bible treats this as normal.

Another view of animals is also explicit in the Bible, however, and gives a different (though not necessarily contradictory) perspective. It is presented most vividly in Psalm 104. There, animals find their niche in creation alongside humanity, not beneath it. Some animals are of no use to humankind—may even be hazardous to human persons. Lions "seek their food from God" and go to bed when humans go out to work. In the sea can be found "leviathan, which you formed to frolic there"

(Ps. 104:26, NIV). Animals, however useful they are to humankind, are supremely valuable to God, who made them in their uniqueness for his own purposes.

As Karl Barth described creation, humankind "is not set up as lord over the earth, but as lord on the earth which is already furnished with these creatures. Animals and plants do not belong to him; they and the whole earth can belong only to God." Thus our responsibility is, not to use the living creatures of the earth for our own purposes, but to rule the earth in such a way as to ensure that all God's creatures are able to fulfill his purposes. In some cases—the whale, the lion—that surely means leaving them to be themselves. Between these two emphases—the instrumental and the ecological—there are many possibilities. On one side are the pragmatic, workaday realities of society as we know it. By this, certain animals are good for food, for wool, for experiments. If this good involves some bad—some unavoidable pain, for example—that is how life often is on a fallen planet, a tradeoff between good and bad, nurture and suffering.

On the other side is the good of the peaceable kingdom, where the lion will lie down with the lamb, and no one will hurt or destroy. So it was in Eden, so it will be in the end—and so we ought to try to make it today.

What both ends of the Christian spectrum share is as important as their differences. Both sides believe that humanity has a unique calling and that our relationship to animals must be worked out within that calling. Christians do not share the modern uncertainty about what on earth we are here for, an uncertainty that adds a wild and flailing quality to secularized debates over animal rights.

A More Peaceable Kingdom

The animal-rights movement would like to change the world dramatically.

Some changes can be made fairly painlessly. We could do without furs, for instance. At some level, though, there is little doubt that animal rights are in conflict with human need. Nearly all scientists say, for instance, that medical research requires animal experimentation. Give it up, and you just as surely give up cures for a thousand diseases. It is difficult to imagine our society giving those up without stronger reasons than animal-rights activists have so far offered.

More likely, a goal disdained by activists will be fulfilled: our society will try to be kinder to animals, even as it uses them and eats them.

The industrialization of food production, global pollution, and the crowding out of wilderness bring new questions about our treatment of animals. Today lions can go their independent way only if we set aside space for them to do so. Whales will survive to frolic only as we restrain our tendency to use them for our ends. God made them; we can now unmake them. One hopes that the animal-rights movement will prod our society to think seriously about such issues.

We can share another hope: perhaps if activists keep asking questions, they will lead us to the realization that no society can be purely irreligious. We must, when asked for the reasons behind our commitments, be able to say more than "science." Scientists who have discovered so many wonderful secrets of the universe have yet to discover an ethic. Science has its ethical commitments, but they are inherited, assumed.

At our society's center, increasingly, is confusion. Having shed Christianity, we have no framework for thinking about ecology, suffering, life, and death—whether for animals or for humans. This void will be filled, perhaps with a resurgence of Christian humanism, or perhaps with something else. No lasting society is truly and fully pluralistic, in the sense of not having any core beliefs. If animal-rights activists accidentally bring this point home, they may do more for humans than they do for animals.

Tim Stafford is a senior writer for Christianity Today _and the author of many books, including_ Personal God: Can You Really Know the One Who Made the Universe _(Zondervan). "Animal Lib" was first published in_ Christianity Today _in June 1990._

■ Open Up

Select one of these activities to launch your discussion time.

Option 1

Discuss these icebreaker questions:

- What is your favorite animal? Why?

- Tell the group about a time you experienced joy as you observed or interacted with an animal, such as a childhood pet, a visit to the farm, a trip to the zoo, or seeing an animal in the wild. What did you appreciate or enjoy about that animal?

- When have you seen someone treat an animal cruelly, observed an animal living in poor conditions, or perhaps acted cruelly toward an animal yourself? What feelings did that experience evoke in you?

Option 2

Pass out index cards so that everyone in your group has one. Take a moment to silently think of your answer to this question: "What animal best matches or embodies your personality?" After a minute or so, privately and anonymously write your answer to this question on your card.

Shuffle everyone's cards and redistribute them. (Be sure you don't have your own!) Read the card you received and guess aloud the name of the group member whose personality *you* think is best embodied by that animal.

After everyone has taken a guess, reveal the correct answers, then discuss these questions:

- What do you see as the main similarities between humans and other animals? What are the main differences?

- What's your favorite animal? What characteristics do you most love in that animal? Why?

■ The Issue

- Do you think animals were created to serve humans, or that God placed humans in the world to care for his creation—including animals? Or do you view the relationship between humans and animals as reciprocal? Explain your answer.

For some, this discussion of animal rights may be the first time you've considered this as a matter informed by Christian faith. This issue is often not part of the agenda of theological discussion in evangelical churches today; it's viewed as unimportant or only an issue for those on the fringe.

"It is too easy to say that we should respect the world as God's good creation without specifying what our obligations to animals are," writes religion and philosophy professor Stephen Webb in a *Christianity Today* article titled "Do All Good Dogs Go to Heaven?" He goes on to say:

> Putting animals on the agenda displaces humans from the center of theology and thus opens a space for the return of God to the pinnacle of religious concerns. This shift does not have to be antihuman, but it can help us to escape the humanism that has infected even the most orthodox theologies of the modern period. To say that God loves animals—and the rest of creation—is not to limit the special moral role we play in the world. To say that God loves only us is surely to reveal our limited imaginations and the self-interest that governs even the most theocentric theological models. Thus, putting animals on the agenda can, among other things, serve to save theology from the distortions of human pride.

- Do you agree that animals and their treatment have been left "off the agenda" by the evangelical church? If so, why do you think this is the case? What do you think of Webb's argument that this matter has serious theological ramifications?

■ Reflect

Take a moment to read Genesis 1:20–28; 2:18–20; Isaiah 11:6–9; and Matthew 6:26 on your own. Jot down a few notes and observations about these passages: How would you put the key ideas in your own words? What stands out to you most? What questions or issues do these passages raise for you?

■ Let's Explore

Humans were created above the animals and given the unique role of caring for them.

In the summer of 2005, the London Zoo posted a sign in front of their newest exhibit, reading, "Warning: Humans in Their Natural Environment." The exhibit featured eight Homo sapiens in a sealed enclosure adjacent to another sealed enclosure of various primates. The human "captives" were chosen from an online contest and spent their time sunning on a rock ledge, playing board games, and waving to spectators. A signboard informed visitors about the species' diet, habitat, worldwide distribution, and threats.

The goal of the exhibit, according to Zoo spokesperson Polly Wills, was to downplay the uniqueness of human beings as a species. "Seeing people in a different environment, among other animals," said Wills, "teaches members of the public that the human is just another primate."

Tom Mahoney, one of the participants in the exhibit, agreed. "A lot of people think that humans are above other animals," he said. "When they see humans as animals, here, it kind of reminds them that we're not that special."[1]

- Imagine you saw this exhibit at the London Zoo. How would you respond? Would it bother you? Do you think of yourself as an animal?

Read Genesis 1:20–28 and 2:18–20.

- Why do you think God created other living beings rather than just humans made in his image?

According to Peter Singer in *Animal Liberation*, speciesism is the allegedly bigoted contention that human beings are more important than other animals. In his article, Stafford highlights the views of Michael Fox who says, "Humane treatment [of animals] is simply sentimental patronage." Further expanding on this viewpoint, animal rights activist Gary Francione goes on to say, "It's not better cages we work for, but empty cages."

- Do you agree or disagree that treating animals kindly but as inferiors is no different from slave owners being nice to their slaves? How might you explain your perspective on the place of animals and humans in the world to an animal rights activist like Singer, Fox, or Francione?

Though Scripture is clear that humans *are* set apart and are higher than the animals, this doesn't give us the green light to treat animals callously or with cruelty. In his article, Stafford highlights a mind-set he *does* view as "pure speciesism"—the point of view which asserts: "Anything that enhances, protects, or increases the joy of the human race is good. Why? Because it's my team." Stafford goes on to say "This is a form of humanism that justifies animal experiments, but a great deal more—too much more."

- Drawing from the Genesis texts, what expectations do you think God may have for the way we are to treat animals? What are some behaviors toward animals that you think are clearly out of bounds for Christians? Explain.

Scripture prophesies an idyllic picture of our future relationship with animals.

Sometimes discussion of animal rights can turn overly idealistic, as if all creatures on earth could live together in peace if only we humans would stop being so cruel! Nothing exemplifies this more poignantly than the recent documentary *Grizzly Man* which tells the story of Timothy Treadmill using video footage he took of his time living among grizzly bears in Alaska. Treadmill loved grizzlies and spent thirteen summers living among them; he felt he'd become trusted by the bears. But in his thirteenth summer, Treadmill and his girlfriend were attacked and eaten by a bear. Much of the tragic event was recorded on Treadmill's running video camera (but is not shown in the documentary).

- Do you know anyone who is overly idealistic about the relationship between humans and animals (either pets or wild animals)? Why do you think they feel as they do?

The Bible portrays the ultimate idyllic descriptions of animals; read it in Isaiah 11:1–9.

- In your opinion, what is the main point of this passage? How is the harmony described in this passage made possible?

- Do you think this imagery (especially in 11:6–9) should be taken literally? If not, what indicates to you that this prophecy is only figurative? If you do take this literally, do you think this means there will be creatures in the new creation? Explain.

Our choices and actions should reflect the care and value God places on animals.

Read Matthew 6:26.

• How is God involved in the lives of his creatures? Does God actually meet their needs? Explain.

• How can we reflect God's character in the way we regard animals? Describe an example.

Stafford points out that when it comes to valuing and caring for animals, "[W]ithin Christianity there is room for tremendous differences—room for the chicken farmer viewing his birds as meat-making machines, as well as for Saint Francis preaching sermons to them."

One response some Christians have to animal-rights issues, particularly to inhumane practices on some factory farms, is to become vegetarian. In his book *Good Eating,* Stephen Webb advocates vegetarianism for Christians. In a review of *Good Eating* for CT's *re:generation quarterly,* Preston Jones summarizes:

Webb's theological case for vegetarianism boils down to the view that post-Flood meat eating was a "concession" on God's part to human sinfulness, that Jesus "announced and embodied . . . a world that affirms life [human and animal]," and that "vegetarianism is not a prerequisite for

Christian faith, but it is a consequence of the Christian hope for a peaceable kingdom, where God will be all in all and all violence will come to an end." Webb is careful not to suggest that meat-eating Christians are second-class Christians, but he does want to say that one way Christians can (so to speak) get a jump start on the coming kingdom of God is by living at peace not only with men but also with nature and its creatures. "Christian vegetarians find the good in what they eat," Webb writes, "not by turning their diet into a new religion but by turning every meal into a plea for the good of all God's creatures."

- Are you a vegetarian or do you know any Christian vegetarians? What do you admire about their choice? What do you agree with in Webb's argument? Or alternately, do you disagree with this linkage between vegetarianism and Christian faith? Explain.

In his review of *Good Eating,* Preston Jones went on to say:

Not everyone will be convinced by Webb's call for Christians to signal their longing for the kingdom of God by refusing to contribute in any way to animal suffering (though in that kingdom lions and lambs will be friends); but his point that factory farms are an affront to God's creation seems beyond dispute. Recall that God informed Jonah of his concern not only for the people of Nineveh but also for their cattle. For my own part, I do find Webb convincing and am now wondering what to do about it.

- Other than vegetarianism, what are actions Christians can take that lesson the suffering of animals? Together brainstorm as many ideas as you can.

- Which of the ideas your group generated (if any) does the entire group agree with as important or worth doing? Which ideas generate a mixed reaction in your group? Why?

■ Going Forward

Form pairs to discuss these next two questions.

Stafford writes that "our responsibility is, not to use the living creatures of the earth for our own purposes, but to rule the earth in such a way as to ensure that all God's creatures are able to fulfill his purposes."

- On a scale of 1 to 10 (1 being abysmal and 10 being terrific), how well do you think the church has done in ruling the earth in the way Stafford describes? Why do you answer as you do?

- How about in your own life? Rate your own care for animals using the same scale. (Keep in mind that though you may not be directly involved in cruelty to animals, you may be indirectly participating in industries that treat animals inhumanely, destroy animal habitats, and so on.)

Review the Do Your Part box below with a partner. Which of the ideas, if any, inspire you to take action? What difference will this study make in your habits, choices or viewpoint regarding animals?

Pray in pairs. First, thank God for creating animals; next, ask God to lead you in any actions you may take to live as a steward of the creatures God made.

DO YOUR PART

Choose one of these ideas, or come up with one of your own, to implement in your own life.

- Do a group service project by volunteering for an afternoon at a local animal shelter or wildlife sanctuary. Do any tasks you can to help out, whether it's interacting with animals or cleaning floors. As you do, commit your work to God as an avenue of caring for his creation.

- Spend extra time this week caring for your pet (if you have one). Observe how you see the beauty of God's creation in your pet; take extra time out to interact with your pet in a way that best fits how God made him or her.

- Try a meal this week that is "cruelty-free." Depending on where you stand on this issue, this could be a vegetarian or vegan meal or you could buy your meat and dairy products for the meal from a local family farm which practices humane treatment of its livestock. You can find a family farm near you at http://www.eatwild.com/products/index.html or at www.localharvest.org.

- If you like your "cruelty-free" meal, consider supporting a local farmer who has committed to humane treatment of livestock by regularly purchasing your meat and dairy products from him or her.

- Consider buying personal hygiene products (such as shampoo or body wash) that aren't tested on animals during their development.

- Consider forgoing fur products; synthetic faux fur is just as warm (and is less expensive)!

- Teach your children to be kind to animals by caring together for a family pet, installing a bird feeder, or observing animals in their natural habitat. Talk frankly with them about the importance of treating animals humanely.

- Invest fifteen minutes in learning more about other current animal rights issues by perusing a Christian site dedicated to animal rights such as www.all-creatures.org or by reading some of the articles found on PETA's Web site: http://www.peta.org/actioncenter/learn.asp. (Though the Bible clearly contradicts PETA's stance that humans and animals are equal, some of the articles on PETA's Web site may inform you of animal cruelty issues in our culture that you were not aware of.) As you read, consider which issues may stand out to you as matters you should act on.

Is caring for the

environment part of

the church's mission?

Genesis 3:6–19

Romans 8:19–22

Acts 14:14–17

THE GREEN CHURCH

■

The church is at a crossroads when it comes to creation care. For decades the world around us has pushed for protecting the environment with the all-familiar call of the three Rs: Reduce, Reuse, Recycle. Yet the church has, in most cases, resisted the beating drum to "save the planet."

Much of the hesitance to participate in the green movement stems from politics getting in the way. Instead of spearheading efforts to protect the very creation God mandated us to care for, many in the church have dragged their feet. But using the *Christianity Today* article "The New Climate Coalition," this study will explore how many prominent evangelical leaders are now calling the body of Christ to wake up and participate in solving this global challenge. Now it's up to you how the church, *your church*, will respond.

■ Before You Meet

Read "The New Climate Coalition" by Sheryl Henderson Blunt from www.christianitytoday.com.

THE NEW CLIMATE COALITION

Evangelical leaders bolster the fight against global warming.

by Sheryl Henderson Blunt

Environmentally concerned evangelicals, including megachurch pastors, Christian college presidents, and theologians, announced their support February 8, 2006, for a major effort to combat global warming.

During a press conference at the National Press Club in Washington organized by the Evangelical Environmental Network (EEN), a new coalition called the Evangelical Climate Initiative (ECI) released a statement signed by more than eighty-five evangelical leaders.

The statement, *Climate Change: An Evangelical Call to Action*, says "human-induced climate change is real," and calls on the US government to pass legislation establishing limits on carbon dioxide emissions—widely believed to be the primary cause of human-induced global warming.

"Millions of people could die in this century because of climate change, most of them our poorest global neighbors," the statement reads. "Christians must care about climate change because we love God the Creator and Jesus our Lord, through whom and for whom the creation was made. This is God's world, and any damage that we do to God's world is an offense against God himself."

Organizer Jim Ball, executive director of EEN, the group known for its 2002 "What Would Jesus Drive?" campaign, stressed the importance of the statement's theological message.

"This is not a political statement being made," Ball told CT. "We are trying to be faithful to the lordship of Christ. It's my commitment to Christ that's driving me. He's said: 'Love the Lord your God with all your heart' and 'Love your neighbor as yourself.' Global warming is going to affect millions in this century, and we feel we just can't stand by. We have to do something about it."

Among the signatories: bestselling *Purpose-Driven Life* author and pastor Rick Warren, World Vision president Rich Stearns, Salvation Army national commander Todd Bassett, *Christianity Today* editor David Neff and executive editor Timothy George, Wheaton College president Duane Litfin, and former National Association of Evangelicals (NAE) president Leith Anderson.

Litfin told CT that some evangelicals have "probably had some blind spots" in responding to environmental issues such as global warming. He said he hoped his involvement would "raise the profile of this issue within the evangelical world."

"I just want to see us more carefully trying to think through: what are the Christian's responsibilities to God's creation? I'm not sure we've fulfilled that stewardship very well, as a nation or as individuals. We can do a better job."

The effort involves a close-to-half-a-million-dollar ad and publicity campaign beginning with full-page ads in *Roll Call* and *The New York Times* on February 9, Ball said. The campaign will follow with a TV spot on Fox News, radio spots on Salem Radio Network, and an ad in *Christianity Today*.

Ball said the group is also planning TV ads on local channels "targeting some specific, traditional states" such as Kansas, North Carolina, Tennessee, and South Dakota—"areas where we know there is good evangelical interest and concern," in order to further boost support for global warming legislation.

Funding for the ad campaign comes from a $500,000 grant the group recently received from the National Religious Partnership for the Environment, Ball told CT. During the press conference Ball said charitable groups such as the Hewlett Foundation, the Rockefeller Brothers Fund, and Pew Charitable Trusts have also contributed.

Evangelical Climate Initiative supporters kicked off the day with a breakfast meeting with Sen. Joe Lieberman, D-Conn. In 2005 Lieberman and Sen. John McCain, R-Ariz., cosponsored a bill designed to create a "cap and trade" system to reduce greenhouse gas emissions. That bill died in the Senate.

While not endorsing a specific bill, the statement calls for federal legislation that would establish emission limits and require "sufficient economy-wide reductions in carbon dioxide emissions through cost effective, market-based mechanisms such as a cap-and-trade program." Ball said he was encouraged by a nonbinding resolution that passed the Senate last year affirming this approach, but "the House is a different situation" and "a good place for evangelicals to make a difference."

Not All on Board

Noticeably absent from the group of prominent evangelical supporters are James Dobson of Focus on the Family, Chuck Colson of Prison Fellowship Ministries, and NAE vice president for governmental affairs, Rich Cizik.

Cizik originally signed the statement, but said his name was withdrawn "to display an accommodating spirit to those who don't yet accept the science on the severity of the problem."

Last month Dobson, Colson, and twenty other evangelical leaders, including Richard Land of the Southern Baptist Convention, wrote to the NAE urging them not to adopt "any official position on the issue of climate change," due to disagreement among evangelicals over "the cause, severity, and solutions to the global warming issue."

Both Ball and Cizik emphasized that the NAE never planned on adopting ECI's statement on global warming. Despite Cizik's absence, thirty-four signers are members of the NAE's board or executive committee, and another fifty Christian organization heads also have ties to the group, according to a knowledgeable source.

Still, many evangelicals remain skeptical of claims on the extent of global warming.

"The evidence is really much shakier than people would tend to see," said James Sherk, an economist and fellow with the Evangel Society, who writes frequently on the global warming debate. The group offers scholarly critiques on current events from an evangelical perspective.

Sherk said the ECI claim that "millions of people could die in this century because of climate change" is "a lot of hype."

"I believe the science on that tends to be more agenda driven," Sherk said. He pointed out that mineral expert and statistician Steve McIntyre of *climateaudit.org* and economist and climate author Ross McKitrick have challenged the findings of the Intergovernmental Panel on Climate Change (IPCC), cited by ECI.

The problem, Sherk said, is "most of the steps they want to take to combat global warming will inflict tremendous economic damage and do very little to affect climate change. . . . We have a responsibility to care for the earth but also have a responsibility to care for poor, and we shouldn't implement policies that would just casually destroy the hundreds of billions of dollars of wealth that could be put to use feeding the poor, aiding the homeless, and providing people with jobs."

Surprising Support

An October 2005 poll conducted by Ellison Research and paid for by EEN revealed that about 750 of one thousand surveyed born-again or evangelical Protestant Christians support hallmark environmental issues like reducing global warming or protecting wilderness areas from development. About 250 say they support these issues strongly. A slight majority of evangelicals, 54 percent, said they believe Christian faith should generally encourage people to support environmental issues.

Ellison Research president Ron Sellers said he was surprised that even 49 percent of politically conservative evangelicals say "global warming is a long-term problem; we are causing the problem today, so we must begin addressing the issue immediately." Sellers also said 44 percent of politically conservative evangelicals would support taking steps now, even at a high economic cost, assuming "that global warming/climate change is occurring, is mainly caused by human actions, and poses a significant threat within your lifetime."

"And that's before any of their leaders have come out and said it's a serious problem," Ball said. "Once evangelicals are convinced this is happening, the other numbers are going to shoot right up."

Sheryl Henderson Blunt is a senior news writer for Christianity Today. *"The New Climate Coalition" was first published online by* Christianity Today *in February 2006.*

■ Open Up

Select one of these activities to launch your discussion time.

Option 1

Discuss these icebreaker questions:

• How were environmental issues addressed in your family, church, schools, or community when you were growing up? Has your perspective on this issue changed since then? If so, how?

• What are the ways (if any) by which your home church intentionally cares for God's creation?

• Why do you think the environment has become a political issue among evangelical leaders?

Option 2

Let's see if you're as green as you think you are by taking the following quiz. Write your answers below, then compare answers with the rest of the group before reading the correct answers together (at the end of this chapter).

• Can you name five well-known animals on the endangered species list for the United States?

• What is the main source of energy the United States uses to generate electricity?

• Can you name the top five countries regarding total carbon dioxide emissions?

■ The Issue

Richard Cizik, vice president of the National Association of Evangelicals, was interviewed for the global warming documentary *The Great Warming*; in his interview, Cizik said:

[T]his newfound passion [among evangelicals], this concern for "creation care" as we call it, comes straight from God and the Holy Spirit who is regenerating people's hearts to realize the imperative of the scriptures to care for God's world in new ways. It comes from God himself. He has changed my heart too. I have had a conversion to this cause. . . . Climate change is real and human induced. It calls for action soon. And we are saying [we must take] action based upon a biblical view of the world as God's world. And to deplete our resources, to harm our world by environmental degradation, is an offense against God. That's what the Scriptures say. Therefore, if we are to be obedient to the Scriptures, there is no time to wait, no time to stall, no time to deliberate.

- In general, how does the environment stack-up when it comes to the priorities of your church? Do you see the type of "new found passion" Cizik describes? Why or why not.

In the last two years, Cizik has been highly criticized by some notable conservative Christian leaders for speaking out on global warming and other creation care issues. In an open letter denouncing Cizik and suggesting he resign his position, signatories such as James Dobson and Tony Perkins said that Cizik "puts forth his own political opinions as scientific fact." The schism between evangelicals regarding the environment stems partly from the political issues intertwined in this matter.

- The environment is a highly politicized and controversial issue in the church, but should it be? Why or why not?

■ Reflect

Take a moment to read Genesis 3:6–19, Romans 8:19–22 and Acts 14:14–17 on your own. Write down anything that stands out to you or questions you may have regarding the passage. At a glance, think about how these passages relate to creation care and the church.

■ Let's Explore

The church must incorporate ecological stewardship into its mission as an extension of the gospel.

The "Climate Change: An Evangelical Call to Action" statement says in part: "Christians must care about climate change, because we love God the Creator and Jesus our Lord, through whom and for whom the creation was made. This is God's world, and any damage that we do to God's world is an offense against God himself."

- In your opinion, is this a fair and true statement? Why or why not?

- "The New Climate Coalition" article stresses global warming as the major environmental problem of our time. What other creation care issues come to mind as those the church could or should address?

- Pope Benedict XVI of the Roman Catholic Church has now been labeled the "green pope" in part by listing pollution of the environment as a new form of social sin that calls for repentance. How does this make you feel? Is it convicting? Explain your reaction.

The gospel is good news for all of God's creation.

Read Genesis 3:6–19. This passage describes the full extent of sin. Not only were Adam and Eve separated from God, but the environment also suffered consequences.

- Have you typically viewed the effects of the fall as spreading to all of creation or just humanity? Explain.

- If the church's mission is to spread the good news that Jesus brings redemption from sin, then how does creation care fit into the gospel? Should it be part of our understanding of redemption from sin and sin's consequences? Why or why not?

- In Romans, Paul describes the creation as longing to be fully redeemed; review Romans 8:19–22. What are some specific examples of the effects of the Fall on the created world? Brainstorm as many as you can.

- Do you think the church loses part of the gospel when it omits the redemption of creation from its message? Why or why not?

The Church can and should point to creation as evidence of God's grace and goodness.

- Are there any dangers if the church co-ops an eco-friendly gospel? If so, what are they?

- In your opinion, would it be alright for the church to partner with secular or government organizations to care for creation? What about partnering with non-Christian religious groups or with those whose lifestyle or beliefs are blatantly anti-Christian? Explain.

Read Acts 14:14–17 aloud. In this account, Paul is preaching to pagans and enlightening them about how God's glory and goodness is demonstrated through creation. Paul used the pagan's connection to the earth as an in-road for evangelism.

- How can Christians today utilize our culture's connection to the environment as a bridge for evangelism? Share specific examples of things Christians could do or say. What affect might this approach have on your relationships with non-Christians?

- What about your church? Brainstorm together some ways your church can harness your community's desire to be more environmentally friendly as a way to point to the redemption Jesus brings.

■ Going Forward

Read the following quote from writer, conservationist, and Christian, Wendell Berry:

> We have no entitlement from the Bible to exterminate or permanently destroy or hold in contempt anything on the earth or in the heavens above it or in the waters beneath it. We have the right to use the gifts of nature but not to ruin or waste them. We have the right to use what we need but no more, which is why the Bible forbids usury and great accumulations of property.

- Do Berry's words seem harsh or fairly accurate? Do you agree or disagree with him? Explain.

- If what Berry says is true, then what bearing does this have on you and your church? In your opinion, is your church overly wasteful?

- Review the "Do Your Part" box below. Which of the ideas would you most like to implement within your church or as a small group? (Put a star by the idea you plan to take action on.)

Take this time to pray together for your church and its role in creation care. Pray that God would show you how to best approach this issue in your congregation.

DO YOUR PART

Bring the three Rs to your church: Reduce, Reuse, Recycle. The church can often do what a household can do when it comes to going green.

Reduce

- encourage your church to reduce electricity, water, food, paper goods, gas, and emissions
- encourage your church to buy sustainable products
- install solar panels
- disconnect drain pipes so water goes into the soil instead of the sewer
- put more information online instead of in print
- give leftover food to those in need instead of throwing it away
- buy hybrid vehicles or convert present vehicles to run on bio-fuel
- switch to energy-saving light bulbs
- purchase energy efficient appliances when old ones need to be replaced
- maintain green space on the property without using pesticides

Reuse

- host an annual clothes, housewares, or furniture swap

Recycling

- spearhead an effort to help your church recycle not only paper, but cans, glass, and plastics as well
- If your church has a building project or remodel in the planning stages, encourage the building committee to use recycled products and green construction in general.

Other

- organize a quarterly community refuse cleanup

- petition the local, state, and federal government to protect endangered species, conserve land, and pass laws that reduce emissions

- spearhead a think tank among churches in your community to discuss how your congregations can address and tackle local environmental problems

- have your church sponsor a community garden and composting site

OPTION 1: QUIZ ANSWERS

Well-Known Endangered Species

Alabama Sturgeon, American Alligator, American Peregrine Falcon, Atlantic Salmon, Bald Eagle, Black-tailed Prairie Dog, California Condor, Delhi Sands Flower-loving Fly, Florida Panther, Gray Whale, Grizzly Bear, Karner Blue Butterfly, Kirtlands Warbler, Mexican Wolf, Mountain Plover, Piping Plover, Peregrine Falcon, Peninsular Bighorn Sheep, Northern or Mexican Spotted Owl, West Indian Manatee

For more information, see http://www.fws.gov/Endangered/media/spotlight. html.

The Major Sources of Energy to Produce Electricity*

1. Coal (49.0 percent),
2. Natural Gas (20.0 percent),
3. Nuclear (19.0 percent)
4. Hydroelectric, petroleum, and other (12 percent)

*most recent data from 2006

For more information, see http://www.epa.gov/cleanenergy/energy-and-you/index. html.

Top 5 Total Carbon Dioxide Emitters**

1. United States
2. China
3. Russian Federation
4. India
5. Japan

Some perspective on these rankings: The United States' emissions was roughly quadruple the Russian Federation.

**most recent scientific data gathered in 2004 for the United Nations

For more information, see http://www.ucsusa.org/global_warming/science/each-countrys-share-of-co2-emissions.html.

■ Notes

Session 1

1. Charles Edward White, "God by the Numbers," *Christianity Today* (March 2006).

2. Vanessa Juarez and David Gates, "A Shepherd Protects His Own Backyard," *Newsweek* (September 5, 2005).

Session 7

1. "Humans Are Ones on Display at London Zoo," *YahooNews*, August 26, 2005, contributed by Sam O'Neal, PreachingToday.com.